That's Not the Help I Need

Real Talk for Women About Winning at Work

Tiffany G. Rosik

That's Not the Help I Need:

From Real Talk for Women About Winning at Work

Copyright © Tiffany G. Rosik (2024)

Published by:

Book Dedication

To my mentors, who saw the best in me, built my skills, and guided me.

To my cookie party friends, who offered endless support via text messages, golf, and happy hours to help me silence the inner critic.

To my parents, the OG believers in me.

To my husband, my constant source of support, even for my most out-there ideas. Sorry, there are no pictures in this book.

To my kids, someday you'll want this advice, so I wrote it down!

And thank you to the friend who encouraged me to write this book and provided helpful feedback at each stage. I couldn't have done it without you.

Table of Contents

You Don't Want to Skip This...

In high school, instead of spending my summers sleeping until noon and hanging at the mall or even making minimum wage working in a retail store, I spent my days working as a golf caddy. I started my day at 5:00 a.m. The best golfers usually played in the morning. Their higher skill level typically meant that the rounds were played faster and with fewer errant shots. My goal was to get a bag in one of the first groups of the day so that I could work two loops in a single day. More casual players filled the afternoons, meaning slower rounds and more work overall. Often the only female in a group of male golfers and caddies, I worked long hours hauling golf bags, ensuring the golfer had the right club at the right time, and doing it all under the hot summer sun. And I pocketed about $10,000 a summer doing it.

How?

By boosting the standard bag fee with an abnormally high amount in tips. Being a female in a male-dominated environment, I knew I had to do more than prove I was a competent caddy. The relationship between golfer and caddy is important, and many golfers at the time were not used to working with a female caddy. So, I took what made me different and used it to my advantage. I showed an interest in their lives and adapted small talk to their rhythm and comfort levels. I learned about the game, but I learned more about customer service.

The better I was at supporting the golfer and helping make them successful, the more I earned in both money and respect. I built a small list of members who would request that I caddy for them in club tournaments and championships, which are very important events to country club golfers. In short, I took the job seriously and showed it in my manners, competence, appearance, and knowledge of the game, and I used soft skills to make connections that went deeper than surface level.

It paid off.

I often earned $50 in tips from one round of golf, much more than my male counterparts averaged. Some of them were not happy to be out-tipped by a girl, but few bothered to ask how I managed to be so successful. They were more interested in being annoyed *with* me than learning *from* me. Their wallets suffered as a result.

Caddying did more than build my bank account. I developed a lifelong love of the game, translating into years of competitive play from high school through university and beyond. I have even worked as a caddy in some professional golf events. I learned how to thrive in a male-dominated field. The relationships I built through caddying opened the door to the college I attended and the college golf program I started. It led to my first internship and my first job after earning a college degree. That first job offer included the opportunity to get a master's degree at the company's expense, which opened more doors for me professionally.

Following my interests, even when they weren't conventional, has helped me repeatedly level up. I've never been afraid to blaze a trail where there wasn't one and to take risks to get what I want. Today, I am the founder and chief executive officer of TGR Management Consulting, advising Fortune 1000 companies on aligning business and technology initiatives to achieve growth. My company is one of the few women-owned tech consulting companies in the United States, and I believe that is one of our strengths.

My success story isn't your typical straight-line ascension via promotion from entry-level job to CEO. Honestly, most modern success stories aren't. The old rules of training for a career and staying loyal to a company for many years don't apply to most career paths.

This is great news for women because the old rules weren't really made for us anyway.

Women face obstacles in their careers in ways that men traditionally have not. As a result, many women who enter the workforce with the same education, skills, and competencies as their male counterparts find themselves stagnating in their careers five, ten, or even fifteen years later, while the men they started out with have moved onward and upward.

The advice in this book is for women who may be:

- In a job they've outgrown but are unable to figure out the best next step

- Overqualified and underpaid but wondering how to progress in their career

- Ready to jump back into the workforce after a change in their personal or family situation—and they don't want to start over

- Trying to make their mark in a male-dominated field and want to figure out the culture to make it work for them

Do any of the above describe *you*?

If you are frustrated with your career's current status and are ready to take bold action to turn things around, this *is* the help you need.

This book was born after years of experiences that were completely and utterly unhelpful or irrelevant to me as a woman in the workplace. I often joked with a close friend and colleague, saying, "That's going in my book." I didn't know it, but she was keeping track and eventually shared the list with me. It was time to put up or shut up and write the damn book.

We all need a little shove sometimes to follow through on our goals. Some extra encouragement to step outside of our comfort zones and take a risk.

That's what I hope to do for you.

I got tired of listening to advice not geared toward women from men whose lived experiences differed vastly from mine. On the flip side, I am also not much for advice that focuses on the inner goddess or books that tell women how to succeed by simply emulating how men do business. I have succeeded as a woman in traditionally male-dominated spaces, not by emulating the men but by understanding how the environment operates and molding my behavior to suit who I am and how I work. Thanks to that early caddy job, I draw many clues from observing and paying attention to details.

Now, I want to share that knowledge with you. I'm here to give you the type of advice you won't get in a typical business self-help style manual. Let's be honest: if following the old rules worked, you wouldn't be reading this book. Career development requires a creative, confident approach that respects your unique circumstances while shooting for the stars. Advice such as, "Consider changing the way you speak to be less intimidating," is not the help you need.

Instead, I will help you:

- Navigate some of the more challenging management styles, including suggestions for making those styles work to your advantage

- Identify opportunities that fall outside the traditional yearly pay raise cycle and strategize the ask

- Decode performance reviews and separate the parts that aren't about you at all from the ones that you should be paying attention to

- Reconsider the traditional method of climbing the corporate ladder and reclaim the term "opportunistic" from its reputation of being a dirty word for women in the workplace

- Seize the opportunity in a layoff so you can bounce back after an unexpected job loss

- Communicate a change in family or personal situation and

- Capitalize on the skills of motherhood in the workplace

And I'm going to do it all true to my personality. I am a direct, tell-it-like-it-is person. I'm not here to coddle, make excuses, or spend a lot of time lamenting the very real truth that women face challenges to success that men often don't have to think about. I like to solve problems, not complain about them, and I believe that to achieve success, you must be willing to take risks.

In return, I ask that you be ready to take action in your professional development by being decisive, assertive, and courageous in approaching the next stage of your career. This book is about stepping into your power as a professional woman and carving out the best path for you.

The 4 Rs

Each chapter will address the main topic through the lens of the 4 Rs: Risk, Rejection, Reset, and Resilience. Surprised to see rejection? Don't be. If being willing to take risks was the only ingredient to success, we would all be successful. We all have ups and downs, personally and professionally. I'm going to demystify the cycle.

Risk: No risk, no reward. We'll discuss how to identify opportunities, calculate risk, and devise a plan to minimize the chance of failure.

Rejection: Everyone faces rejection in their career at some point. If approached correctly, failure is nothing more than a stepping stone to success. I'll provide you with the tools you need to handle rejection in the best way possible.

Reset: I'll help you figure out how to overcome rejection or failure by using the lessons found in defeat to create a new path forward.

Resilience: Most importantly, I'll provide strategies on how to stay strong through it all.

The 3 Key Questions

As you read through each chapter, there are three questions I want you to keep in mind about your own career path.

Why not me?

If not me, then who?

If not now, when?

Insecurity or uncertainty in these three areas holds women back more than anything else, including a lack of experience or qualifications. Overcoming the mental blocks that hold women back can be more empowering than spending more time taking courses, getting more work experience, or trying to orchestrate the perfect circumstances to make your next career move. I believe that perfection is the enemy of progress. Get started, and make adjustments as you go.

My outcome may be unique, but my experiences are not uncommon. As you read this book, I hope you find some light amusement in the stories I present and strong camaraderie in the experiences. We have all been in "that" room. May it empower you to understand and navigate the next challenging situation regardless of what side of the table you sit on.

Your future is bright, and success is yours for the taking. I'm honored to be a part of your journey.

Let's Do This,

Tiffany Rosik

Chapter 1

Managing Up: Strategies for Thriving Under Various Management Styles

Early in my career, I joined a dynamic software start-up. The talent base was youthful and sassy. We were armed with just enough experience to revolutionize how work was done and the restless energy to work the long hours required to be a disruptor in the industry. Our daily operations were chaotic, and the company's direction was in a constant state of evolution. Backed by recognizable investors, we were venturing into an emerging vertical market.

Leadership changes were frequent, occurring semi-annually. Each change brought new tools, methodologies, product features, consultants, and even code bases. We once even scrapped nine months' worth of code to re-train everyone on a new coding language and recreate our previous work in a new code before taking our product to market. With every new leader came a cadre of loyal followers, unfamiliar with the nimble dynamics of a start-up. Every new leader had "a guy" or "guys" (yes, they were all men) that they would quickly usher into key positions to reinforce the direction and tone the leader was trying to set. Most of the imported leaders were from other big companies, and that was all they knew—big companies.

There is nothing wrong with a BIG company. BIG companies are great. They have stuff. So much stuff! Budgets, governance, parties, cake, happy hours and they are not usually in emerging markets. BIG companies also have order of operations, processes to fix things, and expectations on people who perform them. However, leadership on an ocean liner is much different than, say, a sailboat, and our start-up was a sailboat. Not just a sailboat, a sailboat trying to be a world class America's Cup contender!

I had been with this company for about 18 months, equivalent to around five years in big company terms when I experienced the third change in leadership. During the first two leadership changes, I was fortunate enough to continue working with the same manager, a woman I admired greatly. She remains one of my favorite people, so maybe I'm biased about our time together at the company. When leadership changed for the third time, it came with a new manager, Steve. Steve had a distinct management style and a unique type of confidence. He proudly referred to himself as "The New Guy," even going as far as hanging a sign on his office door and introducing himself as such in every meeting to drive home the point. Excited about shaping our fledgling company, Steve hailed from the world of big corporations.

Around three months into his tenure, Steve's big company approach clashed with the reality of our small company's operations. We were approaching a significant milestone set by the Board of Directors, and this time, it felt different and more important than previous milestones. The cubicle farm was buzzing at nearly all hours of the day. The sounds and smells marked the passing hours—bold coffee in the morning, microwave beeps at lunch, and burnt popcorn in the afternoon. Someone once gave me a 1 pound bag of dark chocolate espresso beans. Once.

My peer counterpart Alan and I were lucky enough to have bonus cubes next to each other tucked in the back corner of the office with large windows that often doubled as whiteboards. Our "bonus cubes" were cubicle areas double or even triple the space of the other workstations. They were used to track tasks, design workflow on the fly, create burning issues lists, and even for jokes. We called it the Magic Shop because we were largely responsible for translating the fiction being sold at that time into requirements for a working software product. We worked most closely with the development teams on the detailed requirements. Things moved so quickly that those items turned over daily. There was always a flurry of work being done.

Work was never the problem in this company. The problem was that there needed to be an equivalent measure of output for all the work being accomplished. Much of this was re-work. In the morning, we'd set a path and clarify requirements, only to return the next day when the developers or testers hit a snag and do it all over again. We were like bellhops in an elevator.

Alan and I both reported to Steve. For this crucial board milestone, Steve was tasked with reporting our progress upwards on a near-daily basis. Our communication with Steve was strained, triggered by our tendency to ignore his email requests for updates. It resulted in frequent in-person visits from Steve, usually after we'd missed his emails. Company cell phones and the ability to receive email via phone were a luxury reserved for higher-ups. So, if I wasn't at my desk on my computer, I wouldn't have been checking my email. And I usually wasn't at my desk. I was moving between developers, quality teams, and documentation teams to ensure they were aware of the changes in flight. This was not remote work; it was leg work, and I did it in heels and hose.

During these meetings with Steve, Alan and I would point to the writing on the windows, say some words, and tell him how busy we were, and he would eventually disappear. After a few weeks, he caught on to our pattern and started asking for one-on-one meetings with me to better understand our work. In one meeting, he declared his intention to meet with me every morning to ensure my work was on track. I'm certain it was out of some combination of naivety and respect for authority that I agreed to add my manager's daily status meeting to my already long day.

The next day, we met in his office at 8:00 a.m. He asked me my priorities for the day. I explained them while he wrote them down and then went back to making magic happen. The next day, I showed up in his office at the same time. He took out the list from the previous day and asked which items had been completed. The pattern was repeated daily. If there were six items on the list, it was typical to have two completed, another two not yet started, and one unknown. Some unexpected work may have advanced, while some expected work had not.

Steve and I did this daily dance for about two weeks before I started showing up with my list already written out and ready to hand him so I could get on with the day more quickly. My approach backfired as Steve was getting frustrated with me. He thought I was making excuses for why work wasn't getting done according to the list. He wanted to see a daily to-do list of items neatly checked off the next day. The reality is that Alan and I had no joint strategy for handling this, and we hadn't discussed Steve's daily meeting request with each other at first.

The problem was that Steve wasn't a software guy. He had never worked in a software company, much less in a small start-up. He didn't quite grasp how the immaturity of our software development methodology was creating instability in the design and code work, and I wasn't skilled enough to articulate it then as well as I can now. In frustration, I asked

Alan how his meetings with Steve were going. Alan said he had met with Steve twice but then told Steve he didn't have time for daily meetings and refused to meet again.

I was furious. I was also embarrassed that I hadn't had the courage or conviction to say the same thing as Alan. I felt disrespected at the perception that I wasn't performing at the superior level at which I had always performed and needed someone to manage my every move daily. But mostly, I felt I was being discriminated against. It was one of those pressure cooker moments when mixing stress, exhaustion, and anger ends with tears in your car on the drive home. I was doing as I was asked until I couldn't take it anymore, whereas Alan had simply said no. How Alan responded was not necessarily the right response, but **he was willing to set a boundary that I never even considered setting**. Women don't often stop to think about how best to respond to the request for additional work/meetings/tasks. We just comply (and grumble later).

I never even imagined that saying *No* was an option. I can see now that it is, but being so young and inexperienced then, if someone asked me to do something, I didn't question it. Alan's response was definitely avoidance and could be considered insubordinate, but he probably asked himself, "What would they do about it?" Given our roles, they couldn't outright fire us for saying no to one request, so he let it slide to see if anyone made a big deal out of it. No one did. Honestly, I don't think I would just say *No*, even today, in that situation, but I would offer other options, set a trial period, and then push for change if it didn't work for me.

After a weekend of reflection, I approached Beth, the Vice President of Human Resources (HR) and the only woman at the executive level. She immediately recognized that I wasn't lingering in her doorway to socialize. Expressing my concerns, I didn't label the behavior immediately as discrimination but emphasized the need to stop the daily meetings, which were hindering my work and increasing anxiety. Beth recognized the issue, assuring me that the micromanagement was unwarranted for someone of my capabilities. Together, we crafted a plan for reporting progress more reasonably and appropriately. Beth spoke with Steve, and the daily meetings ceased, replaced by the strategies we developed.

Beth provided crucial support in two ways.

1- **She reassured me that my feelings were valid, even if we didn't label it discrimination, and encouraged me to follow my instincts.** She told me that I was only at the beginning of what she believed was to be a brilliant career, and I would have many more situations in which I would need to follow my instinct confidently.

2- **She helped me articulate my boundaries while still meeting the organization's requests.** Beth walked me through what my ideal manager scenario would look like. We talked about what my prior boss was like (since I really enjoyed working for her). Eventually, we landed on the realization that I needed my manager to give me latitude—we called it *enough rope to run but not enough to trip myself.* I would immediately report critical issues to Steve (by walking into his office) and email him progress twice a week, along with the items on the "to-do" list. Basically, a status report. If there were items on the list that didn't make progress that was unexplained, then it would become a conversation. Today, there is software to help with this kind of tracking, but then, I did it manually in spreadsheets and other documents. Over time, the tools I was using to communicate with Steve became commonplace, with Alan using them as well. Steve still had to make the adjustment to the volatility of start-up work.

Beth's guidance resolved the immediate issue and provided valuable lessons that I carry with me to this day in handling high-intensity, highly visible work.

That was the help I needed.

You may not have experienced the exact scenario I described above, but I'm positive you have your own frustrating story of managing a manager whose style didn't work for you. Managing diverse leadership styles is a shared challenge for many professionals. I was fortunate that my concerns were taken seriously, and the situation was rectified fairly smoothly. However, not every workplace has a Beth to give you the help you need. Instead, I will provide insights and strategies for navigating various management styles and turning challenges into opportunities in this chapter.

My advice isn't to go to HR necessarily and field accusations. It is to find someone you trust with authority who can give you objectivity and perspective. Beth was a trusted person for me who gave me an objective perspective. She could have said, "Tiffany, you've got it all wrong," which is the advice most HR reps give you. I talk about HR often throughout the following chapters, so I feel it needs to be pointed out that HR's responsibility is, first and foremost, to the company. There are great HR reps (like Beth). Still, I suggest that you always be professional when speaking with a representative, and keep in mind that, unlike a union, their responsibility is to protect the organization above all else.

The Five Main Management Leadership Styles

Business books will often spell out the following five leadership styles as though they are set in stone, but the truth is it is rare to come across a manager who fits neatly into one management box. Most people can see a bit of themselves in each style but identify most strongly with one or maybe two at most. No one style is inherently the best or the worst, as each lends itself more readily to different workplace environments. When taken to the extreme, each method can lead to a toxic work environment. The key is to work effectively with a manager of any style, even when it doesn't match your own. I've offered some tips on how to communicate with each leadership style in the last column.

Leadership Style	Characteristics	Strengths	Weaknesses	Communication Recommendations
Authoritarian/ Autocratic	Centralized authority Sole decision-maker Direct, top-down communication Dictate processes and goals	Quick and decisive decisions Strong in a crisis Clear chain of command	Lack of team engagement Can stifle innovation and creativity Can lead to toxic work environments	Direct, concise communications that are focused on getting approval Avoid lengthy discussions and extraneous information
Democratic/ Participative	Open and transparent communication Collaborative decision-making with input from team members	Fosters teamwork and creativity Emotional intelligence and listening skills are valued	Decision-making can be time-consuming and not always effective in high-pressure situations Sometimes only a few people truly control decisions	Bring them on the journey, share your ideas and reasoning Actively seek ways to incorporate their feedback by asking clarifying questions
Delegative/ Laissez-Faire	Team members are encouraged to make their own decisions Hands-off approach to management Horizontal, decentralized communication	Encourages autonomy, flexibility, and skill-building in the workplace Employees take ownership of duties and responsibility for results	Can rely too heavily on self-motivation, leading to stagnation Can lead to confusion over priorities Too much work can be offloaded to subordinates or allow those who are underperforming to "coast"	Take the initiative, but keep them informed with regular updates Seek their advice when you reach a decision point that goes beyond your responsibility area

Leadership Style	Characteristics	Strengths	Weaknesses	Communication Recommendations
Transactional	Most traditional method of management Clear structure with specific goals and expectations Rewards for results, monitoring, and consequences when expectations are unmet	Task-oriented, often effective in stable workplace environments Clear communication from management Defined roles and expectations	Limited ability to adapt to rapidly changing circumstances Can lead to micromanagement Does not foster relationship building and can pit employees against each other	Focus on the specific ways you are meeting their goals and expectations Highlight your accomplishments Avoid making excuses
Transformational	Managers as visionaries who unite the team around a shared vision Four Pillars: Idealized influence, Inspirational Motivation, Intellectual Stimulation, Individual Consideration	Inspirational and empowering communication Use empathy and recognition, encouraging employees to set and achieve their own goals	May lack practical guidance in day-to-day operations with an overemphasis on long-term vision Can lead to employee burnout -Those who need more structure may flounder	Position your work in the context of the bigger picture Highlight lessons learned, especially the ones learned through failure

Conflicts between managers and employees often arise when the management style isn't suited to the work environment's needs or clashes with that of the employee. As you grow in your career, you may also find that what you want and need from a manager may change.

A young, inexperienced employee may prefer a more hands-on, authoritarian management style. Expectations are clearly set out from the start, and there is little chance of making the wrong decision on the job, as the manager makes almost all of them anyway. Over time, that management style may begin to feel stifling as that same employee gains confidence in their abilities and would like to participate more in the decision-making process. A transactional management style with incentives for strong results may work well in a sales-oriented environment, where clear objectives are easily set and monitored but be less effective in a different industry. It is important to look at who you are and where you are in your career as part of the equation for approaching and communicating with your manager.

Toxic Managers

Sometimes, clashes with management go beyond a difference in style preference. Toxic managers do exist, and they climb the corporate ladder quickly if their methods produce the results that upper leadership values. Dealing with a toxic manager is trickier than simply navigating a management style you don't like. It requires a different skill set to handle these types of managers, and sometimes, even then, it's not enough. I would never suggest that an employee should "put up" with it. Still, I recognize that simply quitting or moving on isn't always an immediate option, so having the skills to protect yourself until a better option becomes available is key.

These managers are occasionally more kindly referred to as "counterproductive leaders." They typically prioritize personal ambition and short-term goals over the team's well-being or the organization's long-term vision. They make it hard for a team to work effectively and create an unhealthy workplace culture.

They can also be hard to spot at first. Toxic leaders are often charismatic and well-spoken and have perfected their image when dealing with their superiors. Their short-term milestones are often met, and they can appear to be effectively motivating employees to perform to a high standard when viewed from the outside. They can even seem like a great person to work for until you spend more time in close proximity. Upon closer inspection, their department may have high turnover rates, low engagement outside mandatory tasks, and a generally unhappy work culture.

I once consulted for a company with a toxic senior manager. Jeff was a senior director looking to move up in the company. He also had a protege, who was a very sharp woman. It was a shame that she was learning and being mentored by someone who was emotionally and verbally abusive in the workplace. It was generally known that Jeff was awful to staff below him in the workplace hierarchy, but HR did not have enough details to remove him. Just whispers and rumors. He had a sterling reputation at the company's upper levels as an amazing person and a hard worker because he got results.

Jeff had extremely high, often unrealistic expectations of everyone who worked for him. As a result, people were working essentially 24-7. He would treat contractors as if they were at his beck and call at all times, and people were afraid of losing their jobs if they spoke up about him. He wanted his staff at their desks and ready to work by 7:00 am. In many biotech companies, it is not uncommon to start early, but if he came looking for you and you weren't at your desk, you could expect to be berated often in front of your peers.

I recall an incident with a new employee, Allison, working with me on one of my projects. She is a brilliant woman, quick yet thoughtful and hardworking in getting the job done. When she was only about two weeks into the role, she had a meeting with Jeff. I arrived late to their meeting, only to find Jeff standing across the table from her. I could tell immediately by their body language that the meeting was not going well. Allison was almost in tears, and Jeff was grilling her on her work so far, indicating he was unhappy with it. I entered the meeting and immediately called time out.

I addressed Jeff directly and pointed out that her work was done correctly, perhaps just differently than he had expected. I encouraged Allison to complete her explanation of her outcome, as she had gotten the project where it needed to be, and her timeline was good. I continued in that manner, encouraging her to continue and then massaging the conversation with Jeff to keep things positive. I would ask Jeff questions such as, "Can you get on board with this?" I could leverage the rapport I had built with him in the couple of months that I had been working there to convince him we were on the right path, and he eventually calmed down.

After he left the room, Allison was visibly shaking and distraught at the experience. I apologized to her for being late, as I clearly needed to be there. She eventually got past the experience, but I ensured she would never be alone in a meeting with him. In her case, she had someone in a position to help mitigate the situation, but not everyone is so lucky. Toxic bosses often choose to berate those who don't have anyone who can reasonably protect them in the moment the way I was able to do.

Six of the Most Common Toxic Traits

This is by no means an exhaustive list, but it provides an overview of some of the most common toxic traits managers exhibit.

1- **Arrogance.** An unwillingness to listen to the opinions of others, even when someone else has more experience on a topic. They may insist they are correct even when presented with conflicting facts or refuse to take feedback or suggestions.

2- **Lying, gaslighting, or having inconsistent expectations.** This manager will never take responsibility for decisions that don't turn out as expected. Instead, they may change their version of the facts, make the team second-guess their actions, or keep changing the expectations until they get what they want. Typically, they want results that make them look good or give them more power in the company; otherwise, they are quick to place blame.

3- **Overly competitive with their employees or pits teammates against each other.** This type of manager needs to be seen as the expert. They want to be better than everyone else and, as a result, often feel threatened when a team member is better than they are at some part of their job. These managers may also pit employees against each other rather than foster a sense of belonging and collaboration. The flip side is "playing favorites" by treating certain employees better than their peers as long as they stay on the manager's good side.

4- **Micromanages out of a lack of trust.** When managers only trust themselves and not their team, they have difficulty letting go and allowing their employees to do their work independently. In many ways, Steve exhibited this behavior by insisting on unnecessary daily meetings rather than trusting in my ability to get the work done.

5- **Irritable or explosive.** Employees often feel that they never know which version of the manager they will get from day to day. Often, these managers will give employees "the cold shoulder," make snide comments, or lose their tempers in meetings when they are questioned or when results are not what they expect. Employees fear making mistakes, and their creativity is stifled.

6- **Discriminatory.** A manager that shows preferential treatment to one type of employee regardless of ability is problematic. You may notice that you or your colleagues of a certain ethnicity, sex, religion, or sexual orientation are overlooked for more meaningful or high-level work, recognition, or opportunities, but the reason given is often unrelated. In my opening story, I was unsure if Steve was singling me out because I am a woman or if I was stuck in those meetings because I hadn't had the nerve to say no, unlike my male colleague. Discrimination isn't always easy to spot as it is often covert.

Believe it or not, toxic managers are often tolerated for years. There is usually a culture of fear around speaking up, and individual employees often ignore the behavior to avoid being called out or becoming targets. Others simply move to another position or another company once the opportunity arises.

It happened to me when I provided Jeff's protege, Michelle, with unsolicited advice she did not appreciate. She had just finished sharing information about a change in direction with a team in the UK. The team was asking questions to understand the full scope of the change and its impact on them in particular. With every question they asked, Michelle raised her voice further, to the point where she started yelling. It was only her, I, and one other person in the conference room on the call with the team. They were trying to stay calm on their end, but Michelle accused them of refusing to do what they had been told and that she would report them as being insubordinate. The team on the other end was adept at reiterating their position, but the rest of the call did not go well.

When the other person in the room left, I asked Michelle if I could share my thoughts with her about the call, and she agreed cautiously. I explained that questions were coming from a place of trying to understand the changes, not a rebuke of them. Since it was the first time the UK team was learning about the changes, it was unfair to characterize it as insubordination. Michelle immediately became visibly upset and told me she did not require my coaching or input and stormed out of the room. Less than 24 hours later, Jeff started targeting me. I knew it immediately and why. He started taking a keen interest in the work that I was doing, re-examining every decision, rejecting work that was previously accepted, requesting revisions on unreasonable deadlines, and interviewing team members, trying to surface negative information (which there was none). He then began calling me when I wasn't in the office and sending texts if I didn't answer. He wanted to know my whereabouts at all times, even after hours. I complied enough not to be considered "insubordinate" or in breach of the consulting agreement, but this was clearly retaliatory harassment.

He finally demanded I cancel my travel plans on a family vacation. He was aware of these plans sometime before, and as a consultant, I was under no obligation to change them. He found that unacceptable. I took my vacation AND delivered success for that company, then exited professionally.

So, how do you handle a manager whose style you don't mesh well with or whose behavior borders on toxic? Take the time to recognize the nuances within the management style and understand how it shapes workplace culture. Doing so lets you be deliberate about your approach, understanding when and where to set boundaries and also where to be more flexible.

Risk

Whenever you are faced with a difficult manager, the real risk lies in how you handle the situation—whether you manage, resolve, or move on from it. The approach that I cannot endorse is to do nothing and simply endure it. I only put up with Steve's daily micromanagement meeting for two weeks, which was already two weeks longer than necessary. In that scenario, the manager was "the New Guy," and his approach was vastly different from how things had been done in the past. In addition, the rules were being applied differently to a female employee than to my male peer. Finally, I knew there was a competent HR professional I could turn to in order to solve the problem. I believed that she could be trusted to give me an objective point of view in case I was completely misreading the situation, which I wasn't.

I know that's not always the case. You, as an employee, need to assess the situation and take a calculated approach to address the problem. Imagining that you were giving advice to a close friend will help give distance to the emotion and avoid responding impulsively or making decisions that don't serve your long-term career path. If you are simply dealing with a management style you find unhelpful and not a toxic boss, you may be able to improve your working relationship by being proactive, building their trust, and creating a set of expectations and boundaries together over time.

Build a Professional Relationship With Your Manager

You don't have to like your manager personally or have anything in common with them outside the workplace to have a solid working relationship. Your investment in this area can be as valuable as your work results. The more they trust in your abilities to complete your tasks, your dedication to the company and your role, and your reliability, the better your relationship should become.

Take advantage of your one-on-one meetings (unless they are daily!) to ask the right questions and build trust in your abilities. Focus first on clarifying expectations and priorities.

- What should you focus on right now and over the medium term?

- What types of updates will work for both of you?

- Does your boss want to be informed every step of the way?

- Do they feel that ongoing updates are unnecessary and only interested in the result?

Understanding their expectations more clearly can resolve misunderstandings before they damage the working relationship. If you need more or less direct supervision, for example, don't be afraid to say so and strike a balance that works for both of you. It's important to recognize that these conversations should always come with a tone and temperament that seeks to understand rather than one that seeks to challenge.

I didn't have the skills to adequately explain to Steve that our processes were not linear enough to have clear lists that got checked off cleanly each day. As a result, he worried that I wasn't being effective, and I felt he didn't trust me to do my job. Better communication on both our ends may have resulted in more trust from him and more willingness on my part to provide more frequent updates without the need for daily meetings.

After reaching the upper levels of management myself, I now have a better understanding of the pressure that Steve was under to ensure the company met the milestone imposed by the Board in an industry in which he was unfamiliar. Communicating your interest in the company's larger goals helps you understand where your manager is coming from and what they need from their team. How does your work fit into the larger organizational plan? If you don't know, ask the questions so you get the information you need. It is also a way to ensure your efforts are placed in the right tasks, helping build a better relationship with your manager.

Calculated Risks and Opportunity Cost

This is the place in most career advice books where you are told to step up and ask for more work, volunteer to start a mentorship program or ask for leadership training. None of these are terrible in theory, but all of which, in my opinion, are tactical choices that often add more unpaid work to women's plates without necessarily helping them get ahead in the workplace. Let's be clear. I do not oppose taking calculated risks that pay off in the long run. I *am* opposed to employees taking on unpaid projects that have no long-term career-enhancing benefits.

Sound calculated? That's because it is. It is a very uncomfortable area for women in particular. We often struggle to walk away from a problem we know we can solve. The question we need to be asking is whether it is our job to solve it. How is solving it going to benefit our career? Beware of volunteering for tasks that aren't valued in your workplace and won't increase your worth in the eyes of leadership. Perhaps you think I'm harsh, but research backs me up. A recent study shows that women are 44% more likely than men to be asked to take on "unpromotable work," or work that does nothing to advance their careers, and 50% more likely to say yes when asked.

We'll delve into this topic more in-depth when discussing pay raises and job promotions. Still, my point is to avoid taking on more work to impress your manager, particularly if it is not the type of work that will pay off for you meaningfully. If there is an interesting or relevant project you would like to participate in, go ahead and ask to be a part of the team working on it. Otherwise, you may be better off focusing on being the best you can be at your current job and not diluting your work by taking on extra, unnecessary responsibilities.

Rejection

In most scenarios, the above approach should move you closer to the type of workplace relationship with your manager that allows you to feel valued, respected, and allowed to do your job in a way that suits your working style. That doesn't mean that your manager will change who they are or their inherent management style. A manager with a tendency to micromanage is probably still going to want to check in on you more frequently than you like if you prefer a laissez-faire approach. The key is balance and compromise, reframing behaviors on both sides so you each can see what you get from the other in terms of trade-offs. It's a complementary mindset.

That said, sometimes your suggestions or proposals will be rejected. Often, a manager is set in their ways and not interested in changing for any employee, particularly if either of you is new or inexperienced. People get promoted and must learn how to manage on the job. I did, and I wasn't always great at it early on. Sometimes, despite your best efforts, your manager may not agree with your approach and be unwilling to compromise. If a manager has successfully used their method in the past, they may not be receptive to suggestions.

Handling rejection is always challenging, particularly when left in a less-than-ideal situation. I bypassed the conversation with Steve by going straight to HR, but if Beth had not backed me up, I would have been on my own to handle a micromanager who I felt was wasting my time daily. When your first attempt is unsuccessful, before you *try, try again*, take a step back, and reassess. What is your end goal, and why do you think it failed? There are always lessons in failure once we get past the sting of it, and it is worth taking the time to figure them out before rushing back in.

Start by taking a few days to process your emotions and then create a bullet list of salient points focusing on what's important. I took the weekend to get my emotions under control before heading to HR, and it was worth it. I could articulate my feelings clearly without resorting to accusations or saying things that would have been hard to take back. Ask for feedback in writing from your manager as we don't always remember everything said, but we can review an email. Review your approach and see where you can tweak it moving forward. Don't discount learning from your teammates. When I asked my colleague Alan how he managed the meetings, I learned he had simply refused them! Are there colleagues who seem to be handling your manager's style better than you? Find out how they are thriving and implement the elements that suit you.

Dealing With Toxic Managers

The above advice only goes so far with truly toxic managers. They are often more concerned with their upward mobility than with the people they manage. I strongly encourage you to ask HR for help if a manager's behavior is unprofessional, discriminatory, or creates an untenable working environment. However, it's important to remember that certain people within a company are "mandatory reporters." That means that talking to a certain trusted colleague and asking them to keep it between you may not work and could compound the problem.

In the meantime, you still must work with this person, so maintaining emotional control in their presence is key. When faced with a rejection, reprimand, or unreasonable request, reacting calmly will remove some of the potential for retribution on their part. Remind yourself regularly that their behavior isn't about you and that you control your reaction. Set professional boundaries with toxic managers who may be too interested in your personal life or make comments about topics other than work. Document absolutely everything from inappropriate comments to requests that are outside your job description or anything else you feel may be relevant to remember. Ask for clarification in written form whenever you have the slightest doubt about an instruction or request.

Also, it can be difficult to know in the moment, when it is time to move on. Often, in toxic workplaces, being able to "put up" with this type of behavior can be seen as a badge of honor or a way to bond with other colleagues. Much like having that one bad teacher in school, we sometimes stick out a temporary situation or person we don't enjoy because we know that it's not forever. All businesses have stressful periods, less-than-ideal managers, and other aspects that aren't ideal. Knowing the difference between a short-term scenario and a work culture that tolerates or even encourages toxic behavior is key.

Reset

Many people focus on rejection or failure as the most difficult thing to endure. However, the true test lies not in facing these setbacks but in summoning the resolve to pick oneself back up and move forward after encountering failure. If your attempts to navigate a difficult management situation all seem to result in hearing the word no on repeat, it's time to take a new approach. While formulating how you plan to reset, remember to maintain professionalism in the office. Just as a manager who can't handle hearing no is a drag on the team, so is an employee who sulks when they don't get their way. Your behavior and attitude at work affect your reputation with your manager and colleagues.

Seeking support from trusted colleagues within the workplace or establishing a support system outside can provide crucial emotional support during challenging times. However, a positive support system must offer practical solutions and advice. Going to lunch and complaining about your boss daily only contributes to negative energy and further sours your workplace situation. Putting the situation into perspective is equally vital to avoid letting it overshadow the bigger picture. If, after careful consideration, you find that working with a particular manager is unresolvable, part of the reset process involves preparing to move on while remaining effective in your current role.

Resilience

Resilience is the ability to withstand a difficult situation, bounce back better than before after failure, and adapt in the face of adversity. If you tend to fold under pressure, working on your resilience is one of the best investments you can make in yourself. Adversity is a part of any career trajectory, and successfully navigating it is vital for long-term career success.

Adaptability emerges as a pivotal component of resilience when managing a difficult management style. The capacity to adjust, recalibrate, and thrive in the face of managerial challenges is a testament to one's adaptability. It involves surviving and thriving amidst adversity, leveraging it as an opportunity for growth rather than an obstacle to overcome. The workplace, much like life, is inherently unpredictable. The ability to pivot, learn, and adapt becomes a potent tool in your professional arsenal.

Despite your best efforts, your manager may continue to be difficult to work with. HR may not reprimand a toxic manager, forcing you to decide whether to continue working for them or look for something else. I was extremely fortunate that Beth took quick, decisive action and helped sort out the problem quickly. You may not be so lucky, but you are strong enough to handle any outcome.

Challenging managers, difficult workplace dynamics, and even clashing work styles are frustrating but provide professional growth opportunities. As we navigate our careers, we can often get stuck in our professional rut, preferring to do things the same way over and over. Exposure to different methods and perspectives can take time to adapt to. Consider revisiting the management styles table above to consider the different skills you could try out to move forward.

In Chapter 2, we'll discuss what might be the most relevant and yet least discussed topic among female employees—asking for a raise. Money is not a dirty word; I will help you develop the confidence to ask for what you deserve.

Chapter Summary

- Dealing with difficult managers is one of the most common aspects of corporate life.

- Each management style has strengths and weaknesses and is best suited to different types of workplaces. Working for a manager with the same style preference is not always possible. Adaptability is key.

- Toxic managers exhibit behaviors that belittle rather than support employees, such as micromanaging, pitting colleagues against each other, or practicing discrimination in the workplace.

- Choosing the right approach is the biggest risk—manage, resolve, or move on.

Chapter 2

Crafting Your Compensation Story: Leveraging Your Value Beyond Salary

A recent graduate with a freshly minted marketing degree in 1999, I eagerly stepped into the workforce. Back then, salaries, especially in marketing, weren't exactly hitting the stratosphere. A gentleman I had caddied for over the years offered me a job. The salary range he presented was modest, fluctuating between $27,000 and $32,000–a $5,000 window that was open for negotiation. The added bonus was the promise that I could pursue a master's degree at any school of my choice, in any field, and they would foot the bill. I was fortunate at the time to have another offer in writing, and I had the opportunity to choose. The other offer was for roughly $32,000. I chose the offer that included the master's degree.

The education reimbursement was straightforward–no bureaucratic hoops to jump through. If the school sent a bill for $3,000, they cut a check for exactly that amount, covering everything from tuition to books and even parking fees. It was a pretty good deal.

Fast-forward to the moment I received the job offer, and reality hit. The initial salary offered was at the lowest end of the spectrum—$27,000. I found myself on the phone with the gentleman who had been my connection to this opportunity. With a mix of excitement and apprehension, I nervously pointed out the apparent discrepancy, indicating that the salary was lower than what I had hoped for. I was afraid that it would be taken off the table if I questioned it. I had a lot of pressure from my parents to find a job quickly, and they were eager for me to accept ANY offer. We were not a wealthy family, and my parents were very risk-averse. I also knew that my student loans would come due quickly after graduation, and I had no interest in having to move back into my parents' house after graduating from college.

"I thought we agreed on a range of $27,000 to $32,000, but the letter says $27,000," I ventured. He justified the offer by pointing out that included in the compensation was paying for the master's degree, which was a definite plus. He followed up with a question I loathed, "What do you think is fair?" I proposed $30,000, aiming for the middle ground. Surprisingly, he agreed without a fuss. And just like that, I had successfully negotiated my first job offer–a valuable lesson in the delicate art of advocating for fair compensation.

As I reflect on that pivotal moment, I realize how often women, myself included, underestimate the significance of that base salary. It's not just a number; it's a multiplier influencing everything from potential bonuses to future earnings. The $3,000 difference might seem small initially, but it becomes a substantial factor in the broader financial equation over time. It was also about making the most of the range available. It's true that you may have little negotiating room when first entering the workforce or changing industries, but it's also true that you will have even less once you're in the company. The same goes for jobs with pay ranges, like the one I was working with, where you simply cannot negotiate out of a set range. By making a habit of never taking the first offer on the table, you make negotiation a habit and develop the skill over time so that when the opportunity arises to ask for more, it's (almost) easy.

Here's an example of what I'm talking about:

You accept a job offer at $50,000 annually and don't negotiate for a higher base salary. Over the next five years, you earned a 5% bonus and a 3% annual increase each year. In year 5, your annual salary is now $56,000, and your bonuses have exceeded $2500 for the last five years. Yay!

However, by not negotiating at all, you have left money on the table, thousands of dollars actually. Conservatively, if you were able to get $60,000 as your base salary and the bonus and annual increase percentages stayed the same—you would have $54,200 more at the same point when you consider the $10,000 salary difference plus bonuses and salary increases. That's not insignificant money; it's a car, a killer purse every year, another degree…

I didn't know that my first negotiation would set the tone for my understanding of the intricate dance around pay raises and compensation—a topic that, as women, we often approach with trepidation, yet one that holds the key to our financial empowerment. I believe that you get what you ask for in life, and women have a history of not asking for enough, whether it's time, money, or space. Women have not always been good at negotiating incredible outcomes for themselves. It is a skill that I believe women should be consciously cultivating, as strong negotiation skills are an asset in all areas of life.

This is not an attempt to blame women for unfair treatment in the workforce. Is the pay gap real? Absolutely. Studies show that, on average, women earn less than men, and it's even worse for women of color. It isn't just about numbers on a page; it affects our actual lives—our money, our careers, and our ability to stand on equal ground. Will simply asking for a raise or negotiating more compensation fix the problem? No, but not asking certainly won't get you the compensation and recognition you deserve. We need to take some ownership of the pay gap, too, and not expect the world just to see our value and for a business to voluntarily pay us more. You never have more leverage to ask for more than that first offer from a company.

Yet we often don't because we feel we should be grateful for a job or think they will take the offer away if we ask for more. Negotiating for more money upfront sets the tone that you won't be a doormat for an organization, which is also important at every stage of your career. Discomfort isn't just personal; it's a societal issue that's been around for decades. The way girls are brought up, the subtle messages about how women should handle money—it's an unspoken rule that women should not talk openly about what they earn.

We often think that talking about how much we make is a big no-no, and we are told it's impolite or just not done. But here's the thing: we must start being open about money. It's time to use transparency as a tool to empower ourselves. Negotiating for more money is tricky, especially for women, thanks to these societal expectations. It's like there's an invisible barrier holding us back, compounded by the ongoing problem of women getting paid less than men for the same work. Results of a recent study from the Global Financial Literacy Excellence Center (GFLEC) at the George Washington University School of Business and a group of collaborators found that around two-thirds of the financial literacy gender gap is explained by lower financial knowledge, and one-third is due to lower confidence among women.

Two decades ago, this issue was brought into the mainstream via a book called *Women Don't Ask*, outlining how women don't negotiate for more, have lower expectations when entering negotiations, and are willing to settle for less. Surveys from graduating master's students showed that male students were eight times more likely to try and negotiate a higher starting salary than their female counterparts. Since then, at least one major point has improved: women now report negotiating their salaries *more often* than men. A survey of 990 MBA graduates between 2015 and 2019 revealed that 54% of women reported negotiating their salaries, while only 44% of men did, a reversal of the stereotype that women don't ask.

Unfortunately, women also report getting turned down more often than men when they do. Additionally, women continue to fall short of our overall salary expectations. Research from 2023 indicates that the average minimum salary that women will accept is $66,068, whereas the minimum is $91,048 for men. That's almost a $25,000 a year difference, putting women at a financial disadvantage before they even sign the contract.

So, as we dive into the world of asking for more money, let's break down the discomfort, challenge what society thinks, and embrace open conversations about money. It's time for women to know their value, break through the barriers that hold them back, and demand the pay they deserve. The journey starts with recognizing that the awkward silence around asking for more money can be replaced with a story of strength, equality, and financial confidence.

Risk

At first glance, the risk of negotiating for better compensation may seem like the possibility of failure, being considered greedy, or having the job offer taken off the table. The truth is, the risk lies in NOT getting the best compensation package and paying for it, literally, over the course of your career.

To craft a successful negotiation strategy, women need to do two things:

1- **Think of themselves as a business (I think of myself as Tiffany Inc.).** What is Tiffany's cost of doing business? What does Tiffany need to make to support her costs? Think about your scenario. Do you have a family to support? A house, car, student loans, or hobbies that you fund? What about investing for retirement? Make a list that's specific to your circumstances.

   Before you continue, it's important to acknowledge that most people don't start in a job that can cover everything on their list, but negotiating for even a little bit more can set you up for a better financial future. What could an extra $3000 a year do for you? The purpose is to know what you need to live the life you want to design for yourself so that you continue to move toward it both in the salary and benefits you receive and the investments you make over the long term.

2- **Quantify their value in business terms.** How can you make more money from the buyer of your product? Which, in case you missed it, is YOU! What can you do to make yourself more valuable to an employer? In my first job, the offer of a master's degree paid for by the company saved me money on my education and *made* me money over the course of my career. Can you take courses or programs that will allow you to scale up? What outside experience do you have relevant to your current job or the job you want? More importantly, who do you know in the industry? We often underestimate the importance of the relationships we already have. There are people who can make introductions and open doors for us—all we have to do is ask!

I am not suggesting you spend thousands of dollars to enroll in every program remotely relevant to your job or area of work. As I mentioned in the last chapter, I am not a fan of women adding extra work to their plates that ultimately does little for them professionally. However, targeting strategic upgrades to your qualifications can pay off over the long term. Often, companies offer professional development programs to employees free of charge or at reduced rates. Every decision you make should be a strategic one that you can use to justify increased compensation or to improve your chances of promotion, additional compensation, or a timeline to get compensation in the future. When asking your company to pay for a class or a program, it's important to position it not only for what it can do for you but also to focus on how it will benefit the business. What need will those skills fill? How will you contribute to improving the bottom line?

The "story" you tell on your resume, in your interviews, performance reviews, etc., must be relevant to the business. So many women are overqualified for the jobs they do. If you, as an employee, don't tell your own story effectively, how is your employer going to know? Companies are all about the bottom line. No employer wants to underutilize an employee, so make sure they know your value. This is not the time to be humble or shy about your accomplishments. When discussing your accomplishments, it's not bragging if they are backed up by numbers, so using language like "I answered XX support calls in YY time and positively resolved ZZ issues for the company, increasing customer satisfaction" is an appropriate approach.

Compensation isn't all About Salary

Compensation comes in many forms, with the base salary being only the beginning. However, the base salary is often the reference point for other forms of compensation, including bonuses that are often calculated partially as a percentage of salary, as I learned a few years into my career.

Back in 2005, I held an offer letter detailing the annual salary increase and bonus incentives for my job. It was the kind of letter most employees skim over, but something about it caught my attention. It mentioned a "goal-sharing plan," a tantalizing phrase that hinted at potential rewards for meeting individual performance objectives. The letter explained that under this goal-sharing plan, employees would receive an annual cash bonus based on a percentage of our base salary, which sounded promising. However, the letter didn't detail how the bonus percentage was calculated. It simply stated that it was based on our "base salary" and left it at that. I did some follow-up to ask about the specific percentage and was told it was 3% in the prior years, and they were working on codifying it. I did some quick math and realized that a 3% bonus on my current salary would be a nice chunk of change, and I signed the offer letter.

By the time my first review came and the potential for a bonus, the company had matured enough to produce an incentive plan document outlining the intricacies of the goal-sharing plan in detail. What I discovered was eye-opening and disappointing. The bonus wasn't just a flat percentage of our base salary; it was contingent on a multitude of factors. The company had to hit its earnings per share (EPS) target set by the Board of Directors, we had to meet revenue goals, and we had to achieve certain benchmarks outlined in a scorecard.

On top of that, we as individuals had to meet our Management By Objectives (MBOs), which were specific goals set for each employee. These MBOs were tailored to our roles and responsibilities within the company and were designed to ensure that we were contributing to the organization's overall success. As I pored over the incentive plan document, I realized how complex the bonus calculation process was. It wasn't just a matter of hitting a certain target and receiving a predetermined bonus; it was a weighted calculation based on various factors, each with its own set of variables. For example, if the company hit its EPS target but fell short of revenue, the bonus pool would be smaller, and each employee's bonus would be affected. Similarly, if an individual employee failed to meet their MBOs, their bonus would be adjusted accordingly.

This realization was both enlightening and frustrating. On one hand, it was reassuring to finally understand how the bonus calculation process worked. On the other hand, it was disheartening to realize that my bonus was contingent on so many factors beyond my control. The most frustrating part was the lack of transparency around the process. It wasn't until I received that incentive plan document that I truly understood how my bonus was calculated. Until then, it had felt like a mysterious black box, with the outcome largely determined by factors I couldn't identify.

Despite the frustrations and uncertainties, I've learned the importance of asking questions and seeking clarity regarding things like bonus calculations and incentive plans. I've learned the value of transparency and communication in the workplace and the importance of advocating for oneself in salary negotiations and performance reviews.

Stock Options

Stock options are another incentive that can be confusing for employees. Stock options allow an employee the right to purchase a certain number of shares in the company, typically at a lower price than market value. They often make a compensation package more attractive to a potential employee while being cost-effective for the employer. It is also believed to improve employee retention by providing a sense of real ownership in the organization. In a publicly traded company that has an established history on the stock market, the value of stock options is easier to estimate and is usually a great perk. If the company is new to the stock market, it may be difficult to estimate the value—you'll need to do some homework here to understand the trade-offs and risks.

In small companies or early start-ups, potential stock options are commonly offered to offset lower salaries or weaker benefits packages. It means that you are reliant on forces largely out of your control since increasing the value of stocks is out of the control of one single employee. There is often no value to these options, and future growth is not guaranteed. A 2023 Equity Illusions study of over 1000 U.S. employees with at least a bachelor's degree showed that only 36.4% of respondents understood what a stock option is, and 67.3% were more likely to give wrong answers on equity compensation questions. A fundamental lack of knowledge makes it almost impossible for employees to adequately assess whether stock options are a good idea. Again, you'll need to do some research and ask questions related to the number of stock shares outstanding, potential strike prices, time to convert, etc.

Vacation

Vacation time is often assumed to be set in stone by a company or industry, but that isn't always the case. Small companies, in particular, may not even have a specific policy that applies to all employees and may be open to negotiations for increased vacation or personal days in lieu of stock options or higher pay. For parents with small children or those caring for an aging family member, the extra time off might be more important to them than stock options. The same goes for someone who likes to travel, spend time volunteering, or pursue other passions, or a person who prefers the "work hard, play hard" lifestyle to stocks or higher pay. Some organizations are even moving in the direction of unlimited time off. However, there are caveats to that kind of policy. For example, time off has to be pre-approved, and if you leave the company, there is no pay out for accrued time off because it was unlimited.

Negotiating is a Skill Worth Learning

Fairly early in my career, I stumbled upon a negotiation class from Harvard Law School. I saw it as a chance to equip myself with the skills needed to advance in my career. After convincing my manager of its benefits, I started on the course, not knowing how profoundly it would shape my approach to professional dealings. That laminated document from the course, outlining the mutual gains theory, became my negotiation bible. It provided a framework for every negotiation, from contracts to job opportunities, and it could be helpful for you, too.

There are many negotiation frameworks, but this is the one I learned and found best aligns with my personal style. Some approaches to negotiation don't believe that both sides can "win" or walk away satisfied from negotiations, but that's not my perspective. Don't get me wrong, I like to win, and I enter each negotiation with the goal of walking away with the best deal possible for me. However, I also believe that there should be multiple "winners." When each side feels that they are benefitting from the deal, it lays the groundwork for a better working relationship and additional successful negotiations in the future.

As the title suggests, the mutual gains approach focuses on the fact that in this strategy, each party aims to come up with a deal that is better than any of the original options put forward, trading on what is most important to each party to reach a mutually beneficial settlement. It is different from a win-win in that not everyone will get everything they want. Instead, the hope is that each party gets the most important thing to them while being willing to trade off lesser wants to make it happen, protecting the relationship in the process. The following chart is a very distilled description of how the process works. Still, I recommend delving deeper into the topic and considering taking a course to learn the process in detail.

Mutual Gains Approach to Negotiation

Prepare	Create Value	Distribute Value	Follow Through
Prepare BEFORE you enter negotiations. Clarify your position in your mind before you begin negotiating with anyone else.	What if? The process of inventing without committing, where you propose theoretical scenarios and packages without expecting to commit to them immediately or ever.	Focus on building trust so that negotiations can be as fruitful and open as possible.	Prepare for potential future implementation challenges and devise mechanisms to deal with them.
Try to understand the other party's position as clearly as possible. Read between the lines to understand the reasons behind their stance on certain points.	An exploratory phase of negotiating, where the suspension of criticism is important to get a true idea of the other party's biggest priorities.	Divide value fairly by creating a set of objective criteria that can be used to determine "fair value" in the final package that both parties support.	Include specific provisions for things like monitoring implementation, including specific metrics.
Consider **BATNA**: Best Alternatives to Negotiated Agreements. While it would be wonderful to get everything you want, that is unlikely to happen in most negotiations. What would be the best alternative? What would be the best alternative for the other party?	Using your creativity to propose different bundles or package options combining multiple areas of importance is an opportunity to test out various possibilities without committing.	Keep at least two "packages" on the table when negotiating.	Include communication and conflict-resolution provisions.
Prepare alternative options for both parties before negotiating begins. Be able to articulate the other party's position and your own to show that you understand where they are coming from.	This generates opportunities across both parties by trading on possibility.	Settling on a package that may not include everything either side had hoped for but that both sides feel is fundamentally fair helps support implementation and safeguards the relationship.	Continue to work to improve the relationship between the parties to aid in future negotiations.

46

Rejection

Sometimes, despite the best preparation and effort on your part, you won't be able to get the salary or compensation that you ask for. In some cases, it might be a matter of policy not to negotiate, or there could be a salary range beyond which the amount is not up for negotiation. Or you might simply be turned down. Unfortunately, the data shows that, in general, women tend to get turned down more often than men when negotiating salaries. Worse, they can even face backlash.

Handling rejection professionally when negotiating a salary and compensation package, particularly with a new job offer, is key to maintaining a good professional relationship with your employer. When handled well, it can also help start negotiations positively the next time you try.

1- **Don't take it personally.** Rejection hurts, and it can be a bit of a blow to the ego to feel as though your skills aren't valued enough to secure a better compensation package. There are many reasons for an employer to stick to a lower deal, not the least of which is that they always look out for the bottom line.

2- **Always ask for feedback.** In the case of my first job, the initial job offer was at the lowest end of the pay scale. Instead of simply accepting that, I asked why and learned the rationale was that they thought that the master's degree offer was worth the trade-off. Understanding where the employer is coming from can either help move a negotiation forward, which was my experience, or it can help you understand what types of things you can do to change their mind in the future.

3- **Get it in writing**. Not to trap anyone but to ensure you do not forget or misunderstand anything. Written communication lays things out more clearly and invites less confusion. This is especially helpful if you are making an agreement with one person (a manager) and someone else (HR) is responsible for putting the documentation together. A simple email outlining a verbal agreement will add clarity.

4- **Set a goal.** My first employer could have said that the salary was open for renegotiation once the master's degree was completed, after a six-month probation, or if I met certain targets. Once you have feedback, set a goal for what needs to be achieved before trying to negotiate a second time.

5- **Have a timeframe for achieving it**. The longer you go at a lower base salary and compensation package, the more likely you are to get complacent about it and the less urgent a new negotiation session will seem.

6- **Create a backup plan.** Let's say you do everything on this list and still cannot negotiate a better deal. Then what? Decide before you head into negotiations so that you know the next steps to take if you are unsuccessful.

Resilience

There's no doubt that an unsuccessful negotiation can take an emotional toll, and having to wait for the next opportunity to negotiate can be tough. Recognize if you tend to self-blame or engage in negative self-talk. Work on building your confidence and maintaining your determination even after a negative negotiation. Resilience is about mental toughness and the ability to bounce back from adversity. It's important to separate your emotions from your professional behavior. Starting a new job with a negative aura of disappointment is the worst way to make a first impression. Consider the feedback you received as room to grow, and put the steps from above into action.

Engage the skills of proactive problem-solving. It takes time to prove your worth, particularly if you are just starting out or switching companies or industries altogether. Work on building your professional portfolio, and consider enrolling in a negotiating skills class as I did. Practice the techniques and have the skills and experience to support your requests. Build those professional relationships and prove your worth through your work. Reflect on lessons learned from the negotiation experience, including strengths and areas for improvement, to inform and shape future negotiation strategies for greater effectiveness.

Reset

There is more than one way to reset following a disappointing negotiation. The first is rather immediate. Many people worry that an offer could be taken off the table if they negotiate too strongly, but few realize they are also entitled to walk away. Obviously, this is contingent upon already having a strong alternative, such as a job you can simply choose not to leave or a competing offer available. It might not be realistic for everyone, but if it is for you, keep that in mind during the process. If you feel that the company is too rigid from the start, it may be better to choose a different path.

The second is taking the lower offer and then dedicating yourself to preparing for the next opportunity to negotiate higher pay by developing a plan to strengthen your case and get what you plan for. Follow the steps in the sections above to build a strong argument for why you're worth more and how it can benefit the company's bottom line.

Finally, accept the deal but prepare for your exit. If turning down the job isn't in your best interests but you don't see the possibility of negotiating very much down the line, use the time at the job to build an even better professional profile and gain more experience before moving on to the next, better opportunity.

Seemingly small details can have a significant impact on one's career trajectory. It's about more than just numbers on a paycheck; it's about empowerment and strategic decision-making in the workplace. And it's a skill that anyone can learn and use to their professional advantage.

Chapter Summary

- In life and business, women must proactively ask for what they want. Negotiating a better base salary and compensation sets the stage for a better financial future.

- When negotiating, consider yourself as a business and quantify your value in business terms. Tell an effective story by emphasizing what you will contribute to the bottom line. Show your value.

- Be prepared before you negotiate. Consider taking a negotiation class or at least read up on the topic and prepare your approach in advance.

- Get feedback in writing and identify the next steps.

- Have an exit strategy should future negotiations not meet expectations.

Chapter 3

The Problem with Performance Reviews: The Gap Between Perception and Reality in Performance Feedback

Performance reviews—two words that can universally deflate any room. It doesn't matter what room you are in or what job you have, nor does it matter what fancy name your company calls it or the level of formality by which it's undertaken. Whether you are the giver or the receiver of the review, there are equal parts of annoyance and anxiety in completing them. It is hard to come up with the right words that demonstrate confidence without being arrogant or narcissistic with a dash of self-effacing focus on improvement. It is commonly understood that less than actionable dialogue will be exchanged, and salaries will be adjusted by obtuse formulas that are hard to rationalize.

For inexplicable reasons, I saved a number of my performance reviews, printed them out, and neatly stored them in a filing cabinet in my home office. I recently found some motivation to clean out that time capsule and re-discovered them. As I read them, I had three observations:

1- **I was my own worst critic** and lowered my own score through keen self-evaluation. It was the equivalent of leaving answers blank on a multiple-choice test. I consistently underscored myself by 1 point compared to how my peers scored me and a full two points lower than how my leaders scored me.

2- **The comments didn't reflect the scores** in the few areas where I received lower scores from my peers. For example, I received a 7 out of 10 in the Development Potential category, yet my peers' comments were "Exceptional" and "Works hard to stay at the top of the game." Nearly every time, the written comments were a glowing (and contradictory to the score) endorsement. I now realize that, unfortunately, this is quite common in women's performance appraisals. In the study "Potential" and the Gender Promotions Gap, 30,000 management-track employees at a North American retail chain showed that, on average, the female employees received higher performance ratings yet scored 8.3% lower in potential than their male counterparts.

3- **The overall numerical average had little impact on money**, bonuses, or title promotion. It was largely based on the flowery words my manager wrote that could be carried forward to a Senior Leader.

I had grown immensely professionally in the two years of working for the small software company from Chapter 1. My ability to continuously create the capacity to perform the additional responsibilities being lobbed my way seemed endless. During that time, my husband and I both were putting in the hard time building our careers and our relationship. There were many evenings spent on the couch with dueling laptops and beverages. More than a few dinner deliveries were eaten in my office while driving to a deadline.

At some point in the office, I paused to look around and found that I was the only one in the Magic Shop. My counterpart had disappeared. I would see him around and knew he was working, but he wasn't keeping my pace. I was outworking him, and it was great! I was out in front and putting distance between us. I loved it. However, I wanted to be compensated for my exceptional work performance. So, I drafted my justification for a pay increase and practiced my pitch. In my next meeting with my manager, Steve, I presented it to him, using all my carefully crafted words in my rehearsed tone.

Crickets.

It turned out that Steve was not prepared to talk to me about salary. I didn't tee it up for him. I just hit him with it. In golf terms, I tried to hit my driver off the fairway and duffed it. After several very long moments, Steve informed me that mid-year raises are not common. Budgets are set due to _____ (insert reasons here). Still, we left on a positive note after he told me he would consider it. I nodded, thinking, "That seems reasonable. I did spring it on him and all."

A few days later, Steve and I sat down again in his office and he broke the bad news to me. HR said we couldn't do that, and I had to wait for a review cycle when salary increases could be considered collectively as part of the revised budgeting process blah, blah, blah. Honestly, I stopped listening. I had gotten rejected and was already licking my wounds before I even left his office. Instead, I went back to work and continued at my pace because it was what needed to be done. I had a job to do, and I believed the team and my company would win when I was successful.

Performance reviews came around again. UGH. By comparison, my career was in its early childhood years, so I had yet to have many of these review opportunities. This particular review form had four questions and a section for manager comments. The questions were:

1. What accomplishment or performance are you most proud of?

2. What strengths do you bring to your role?

3. What areas do you see room for improvement?

4. What are your future goals?

Using much of the work I had already prepared from my prior attempt to negotiate a pay increase, I made a few tweaks and dropped my answers in the template. Under future goals, I gave my justification for a pay increase. When I felt confident in my words, I emailed the form to Steve and showed up in his office a few days later to discuss my review. He gently told me that while it was well-written, I was unlikely to get a pay increase based on my responses. He explained that my work was valued and undoubtedly successful, but it was not easily translated to Leadership.

What did that mean? I needed to speak in the language of the C-Suite and tie the work I was doing directly to the company's strategic goals in quantifiable terms. He pointed to the printout pinned to the board behind him, then reached over, grabbed it, and handed it to me. It was a 1-page printout of the company's annual goals that had been presented organization-wide several months prior. We sat together over the next hour, discussing my work and the strategic goals. We crafted statements like "Drove the development of X number of user stories representing Y% of expected MVP development." I then had to go back, run the reports, and capture the accurate information. We worked on it two or three more times until each of my responses to the four questions had clear and specific data aligned with each of the strategic goals.

If you recall, Steve and I had a rocky start to our manager-managed relationship. He could have shrugged his shoulders when I turned in my initial performance review and just sent it off to HR. He didn't. He was earnest in his dedication to developing my skills. I've learned many valuable lessons in my career, yet this one sits at the top. The experience taught me to pay attention to a company's strategic goals.

- Ask for them

- Ask how the company has previously performed against them

- Pay attention in company meetings when they are reporting their performance against them

- Make sure my job function has a direct tie to more than one of them

If I can't tie my accomplishments directly to the company's revenue or a strategically significant milestone, they can't tie my revenue (salary) to it either. I didn't learn about that last one from Steve. I learned that lesson the hard way (see Chapter 5).

It was the help I needed.

Performance reviews are such an ingrained part of business culture that they are often considered one of the definitive measures of an employee's success in their job. Pay raises, bonuses, and promotions can hinge on the annual or semi-annual performance review results. According to HR Magazine's article "Performance Review Problem," they are so commonly used that around 71% of companies use some version of them to assess employee growth and success. The problem is that while the review system hasn't changed much over the last 50 years, the way businesses work has. Not to mention, 45% of managers feel that performance reviews bring little, if any, benefit to their company, and 24% of employees report being ready to quit their jobs over an ineffective review.

There are myriad criticisms of the process. Workplaces have changed, and with it comes fewer full-time, in-office employees who remain in the same position or company for years. Hybrid working conditions, including full- or part-time remote working and collaboration with freelance workers or consultants, can make it difficult for managers to observe some of the metrics traditionally used to evaluate performance. Modern businesses have many more moving parts than they used to. Companies are aware of the problem yet are not always clear on how to fix it. In the same HR Magazine article, a survey of over 800 firms indicated that only 26% felt their performance review systems were effective and admitted needing to be adjusted to be more accurate and objective in several areas.

My biggest concern with performance reviews is how often **the feedback is more about the person giving it than about the person under review**. Trying to summarize everything from the past year in a single interaction, like a survey or meeting, is not the most effective or objective way to assess job performance, and the lack of training and guidance around how to maximize your review (or even review a peer) is almost non-existent.

Risk

Dissecting the Subjectivity of Reviews

The risk in these feedback mechanisms for you, as the employee on the receiving end, is that a manager's expectations and perspective on your performance are often subjective and not necessarily an accurate reflection of your true strengths and potential. As an employee, **you must find a way to manage those expectations while also being able to separate the useful feedback from that which ultimately doesn't serve your professional growth**. Managers may interpret criteria differently, be influenced by personal biases, or have varying expectations based on their experiences and perspectives. Two individuals with similar performance may receive vastly different evaluations based on who is assessing them.

Performance reviews often rely on metrics and criteria that may not fully capture an individual's contributions or capabilities. Quantifiable measures such as sales targets or project completions add some objectivity to the process but may still overlook less tangible but equally valuable qualities like teamwork, innovation, or adaptability. Such a narrow focus can disadvantage employees whose strengths lie outside traditional metrics and fail to provide a comprehensive assessment of their performance. Factors such as personal relationships, office politics, or implicit stereotypes may influence how an employee is perceived and rated, regardless of their actual outcomes.

Women tend to have more operational responsibilities that are not easily tied to metrics. It is important to recognize that and work to change it. Doing so could mean working with your manager to quantify your work and tie it to the strategy or bottom line or reducing the amount of unquantifiable work you are responsible for completing. An office manager is a great example of an operational role; there is a way to tie that work to the bottom line. It's more difficult for a project manager. Still, if you run a project on time and within budget, you should be able to make quantifiable statements that tie to strategic objectives. A significant part of my career has been in non-revenue generating roles, like Project Manager and Program Management Office Director. In those roles, I had to tie my contribution, as well as my team's, to the company's overall goals. I had to quantify my impact on those goals and then reframe the conversation to "my value," not my cost. The value is usually found in the costs you helped the company avoid through risk mitigation and efficiency AND the additional capacity you created for others by avoiding those risks and reducing rework.

Managing Expectations

It's important to learn strategies to manage your expectations around performance reviews. They come with such inherent limitations that a failure to set realistic expectations can result in personal disappointment and strained work relationships. Performance reviews have some value but can never capture the full picture of your abilities and contributions to the company. Instead of solely focusing on the final performance review rating or score, **focus on the importance of the feedback and development opportunities provided throughout the evaluation process**. Try to see it as a continuous learning opportunity rather than a judgment of worth.

Seek clarity and specificity from your manager. Performance criteria can veer into vague, generic categories that don't offer concrete avenues for improvement. When in doubt, ask for clarification and then **focus on one or two actionable items that you feel will benefit the company and your professional development**. If relevant, set timelines and milestones to track progress objectively. As I mentioned earlier, **tie your achievements to one or more of the company's strategic goals and highlight your contribution to meeting them using clear and direct language**.

Embrace constructive feedback. It can sometimes feel as though performance evaluations are a "you against them" type of activity, but even for all their flaws, they are an opportunity to see yourself through your supervisor's eyes and identify areas for improvement. **Not all feedback is useful or accurate**, so rather than reacting to it immediately, take some time to allow the emotions that come with criticism or negative feedback to dissipate before sifting through it for the nuggets that you feel are accurate and most relevant to your future growth.

Rejection

As my personal story highlighted, performance reviews can be ineffective or not, leading to expected outcomes even when you are performing above expectations. Performance reviews are often about corporate performance expectations, management agenda, or personal bias and are not necessarily based on your skills. I believed I was crushing my work goals. Yet, it wasn't translating on the review, partly because of how it was structured and partly because I wasn't effectively communicating my accomplishments in a way that showed my true value to the company. A supportive manager dedicated to helping me develop those communication skills made a difference. Still, if Steve hadn't been willing to help me understand the system's nuances and craft a better narrative of my successes, the outcome would have been much different.

To be completely transparent, I *was* disappointed I didn't get more money. My expectations were a lot higher than what my manager could get for me. He was extremely excited to share with me that he had been able to come back with a higher amount like we had planned, but I took the wind from him with my reaction. I was too young and inexperienced to understand how hard it was to get additional money for your team members, and my reaction was not what he had expected. When I became a manager, I lost more of these battles than I won, but I always fought hard for my team. I understand better now how hard Steve had fought for me and how successful he had actually been.

Negative performance appraisals or even mediocre ones that don't translate to the type of recognition or compensation hoped for, can be crushing in the moment. A staggering "50% of employees did not expect their performance review rating, and 87% experienced a negative surprise when they received their rating." A study of 1500 employees revealed that 18% of women and 26% of men reported crying following a negative performance review.

I included that last point here as a reminder that these ratings, as much as they are supposed to be objective and reflective only of our professional accomplishments, can still feel like a personal attack and affect us deeply. I also include it because I know that sometimes, when women cry, we or others may feel that it's a feminine display of emotional instability or weakness when the truth is that men are affected and cry as well. Getting emotional about a performance review is normal. Still, you need to get tactical about your response.

Begin by taking a day or two before looking back at the review to distance yourself and be able to read the feedback again with a critical eye. There are always lessons to take away, even if, as in my case, they are less about your performance and more about how you present it to your superiors. Which parts of the feedback ring true, and which parts can you safely move to the side and ignore for now? Are any parts completely false or potentially harmful to your career, and not just unhelpful? Those should be addressed directly as soon as possible. If you couldn't discuss your review or feel that you were too emotional to address your concerns accurately, ask for a follow-up meeting and prepare your questions and concerns in advance. You could also ask to provide an additional rebuttal in writing.

Resilience

Resilience, within the realm of performance feedback, can be defined as the ability to recognize, accept, and adapt to discrepancies or inconsistencies in the feedback received from different sources. Performance feedback may vary depending on the evaluator's perspective, but resilience empowers you to leverage the feedback constructively to fuel personal growth and development. Parsing out relevant feedback from noise involves discerning between constructive criticism that offers genuine opportunities for growth and irrelevant or biased critiques. Focusing on specific, actionable feedback that aligns with your professional goals and performance objectives and the company's performance targets can help you prioritize which feedback to incorporate into your development plans.

Despite doing everything right, you may still walk away dissatisfied with the final version of your review or with being passed over for a raise or promotion. If your company ties these things to annual reviews, it can be tough to accept that you will have to wait until the next formal evaluation period comes back around to have a second chance at moving up professionally. Seek support and guidance from a trusted mentor, colleague, or supervisor who can offer valuable insights and perspectives. I know that I would eventually have figured out how to craft the right narrative on my performance reviews to get the recognition and compensation I deserved without Steve's help, but having him help me the first time around saved me a lot of time and effort, not to mention lost opportunities and missed pay increases. Being resilient doesn't have to mean going it alone.

Reset

Resetting means figuring out how to move forward over the short term and setting one or more goals for the upcoming year in your current role in the company. Keep the larger career path and your longer-term goals in mind, and then break them down into yearly goals that can be achieved within the company's forced performance framework. Early in my career, my BIG career goal was to be a CIO or CTO with a corner office and giant glass windows, and I could wear power suits to work. These goals may seem silly now, especially given the changes in work locations and attire, but that was the picture in my head for years. The important point for me back then was, How does a lowly business analyst get the skills to eventually make the biggest technology decisions that drive the company forward and make the company recognize that?

The response will depend on the structure of the performance review and the growth structure of the organization. At that lower level, a significant portion of the evaluation will likely be focused on measurable tasks. Receiving ongoing feedback, both formal and informal, to be able to course correct and adjust goals between review periods is key. You'll need to seek ways to incorporate unconventional or innovative approaches to non-measurable or difficult-to-quantify work. Incorporating one or more of the approaches below into your ongoing strategy can help management see your value throughout the year and provide you with concrete examples to use when the next performance review comes around.

Some Alternatives to Traditional Performance Reviews

Mentoring

Mentoring relationships can address various professional development needs, including technical skills, leadership abilities, industry knowledge, communication strategies, and interpersonal skills. Mentors draw upon their own experiences, insights, and expertise to provide guidance, feedback, and encouragement. Mentors serve as trusted advisors and role models.

It can be used as an alternative to formal performance evaluations or as a complementary practice, offering a personalized approach to supporting professional growth and development. Mentoring prioritizes ongoing learning, feedback, and mentorship relationships to drive continuous improvement and career advancement.

Finding a mentor, however, can be daunting if you can't think of someone immediately at your place of work to approach. This is one case in which the person seeking out the mentor needs to be proactive and engaged in building a long-term relationship with someone. Having realistic expectations of what a mentor can help you achieve is also essential. **Mentors are not magical problem solvers.** However, they can offer insight into things like leadership decision-making.

Before approaching someone to be your mentor, you should first determine your needs. What exactly are you looking for from a mentor? Then, identify potential mentors within your current professional network or who you know in other capacities but who possess the qualities and knowledge you seek. If you can't identify anyone suitable, consider joining a professional organization to expand your contacts, reaching out to mentorship groups online, or even asking a trusted person if they have someone they could recommend.

Next, prepare your introduction. It's important to be upfront about what you are looking for, the time frame involved (short or long-term mentorship), and how often you would like to be in contact. Consider whether you prefer in-person, phone, video, or email correspondence. Giving the other person a clear idea of the commitment can help them make an informed decision and avoid disappointment. **Once someone agrees to be your mentor, take the initiative to build the relationship and take responsibility for ensuring that plans are made, you have clear goals and objectives for your meetings, are punctual, interested in their feedback, and prepared to put in the work.**

Skills Development

Skills development initiatives can complement traditional performance evaluations by providing a proactive and dynamic approach to enhancing employee capabilities and effectiveness within organizations. Skill-based initiatives and training programs offer quantifiable and transferable competencies needed to excel in current and future roles.

The negotiation course I took was something I enrolled in following a performance review with a manager, and it has been extremely useful to me professionally ever since. Use the specific and actionable feedback from the performance review to target skill development opportunities that will help you grow in the current role and prepare for the next role.

Feedback, Performance, and Future Chat

The "Feedback, Performance, and Future Chat" assessment involves a conversation between an employee and their supervisor or manager to discuss various aspects of the employee's performance, provide constructive feedback, and outline goals and development plans for the future. It emphasizes open communication, collaboration, and mutual understanding between employees and their managers to support continuous improvement and career development. Ideally, these types of conversations should happen quarterly.

It is a great way for employees to get consistent, regular feedback between formal reviews and a strategy to get beyond some of the incorrect or unhelpful feedback you may have received on a performance review. Regular dialogues of this nature help ensure that your contributions remain visible throughout the year, especially in larger organizations where managers oversee numerous direct reports. This collaborative approach enables you to set realistic yet ambitious goals and devise actionable plans to achieve them. It is particularly valuable because it emphasizes fostering open and honest communication. You should be encouraged to ask questions, share perspectives, and provide input, ensuring that the feedback received is relevant and constructive and helps keep the focus on where you are headed and how you are evolving to get there. If this has not been your experience, you should own the conversation and drive for this outcome. Let's be honest: there's no real training for someone to become a manager, and it's likely a manager doesn't know how to lead this conversation, so be opportunistic. Lead it. Follow up on it. Control the conversation.

360-Degree Performance Appraisal

The 360-degree performance assessment process is a comprehensive method of evaluating an individual's performance by collecting feedback from multiple sources, including supervisors, peers, subordinates, and sometimes external stakeholders such as clients or customers. It provides a more holistic and well-rounded view of an individual's skills, competencies, and behaviors, as it considers perspectives from various angles within the organization.

This is another tool for getting past poor feedback. If your company doesn't have a 360-degree review process, ask your manager to approach a few people you worked closely with to get their perspective or have them communicate directly with your manager. Be careful not to influence the conversation; otherwise, it's not objective and could be considered triangulation, which is also not good for problem-solving.

Chapter Summary

- Performance reviews are imperfect assessments of an employee's skills and performance and sometimes reveal more about the assessor than the employee being evaluated.

- Tie your accomplishments directly to the company's revenue or a strategically significant milestone.

- Learn to separate legitimate, constructive feedback from feedback that is not helpful to your career development.

- Seek out guidance, support, or mentorship from your manager or someone else whose professional opinion you trust and respect.

- Don't get overwhelmed by focusing on too much or looking too far down the line. Identify one or two goals that you can accomplish in the next year, and focus your energy there.

Chapter 4

Understanding Pay Raises and Promotions: Setting Yourself Up for Success

In my career, I've been fortunate to have worked for truly phenomenal leaders. They were "Servant Leaders." These types of leaders focus on building relationships and developing the leadership skills of their employees rather than simply looking out for the best interests of the corporation. The leaders I benefited from working for were people builders and champions of my work. They fought for my recognition, pay raises, and promotions and were responsible for significant leaps in my career advancement. They were both women.

Surprised? Over my professional life span, women's leadership has evolved positively. There are now more elevated opportunities for women. It's no longer 100:1 for that VP title.

The first female manager I reported to was Caryn. She was responsible for bringing a new software product to market while managing a legacy software product long enough to make the other one happen. She was sharp, capable, and clearly overburdened with work in both lanes. She had years of experience as a user of similar software tools to my months of experience in software development and a fancy degree. Over the next year, she invested thousands of hours in me, brain-dumping her user experience and providing me with significant on-the-job training.

She would walk through the business workflow with me, and I would attempt to match the system workflow on adjacent walls. When I got it, she would send me off to translate it into technical requirements. The two of us would iterate that way for weeks until there was enough content to make client visits to get real-time feedback. Caryn intentionally took me to our toughest, most vocal clients to present our work. The first visit was as brutal as she had promised it would be. I was not prepared to hear how they would call our baby ugly! That meeting was an education of a different sort, but Caryn was masterful. Her ability to focus their criticism and guide it to constructive and actionable information was an indelible experience.

Over the next few months, Caryn transitioned more of that work to me so I could run independently on both product lines. She was being pulled into other directions by senior leadership but always made time to whiteboard a workflow issue with me that the development team had bounced back. One morning, she came into the office in a flurry and asked that I join her in her office. It was one of those sinking feelings like I had suddenly been summoned to the principal's office. A mix of "Oh, Shit" and "What did I do now?"

I grabbed my usual seat under the whiteboard at the mini table. Caryn spun around on her chair and wheeled herself over with a stack of papers. Her hands were carefully folded over the paper as she nervously told me her news. She was pregnant. Unexpectedly so. And, most relevant for me, heading back to Atlanta to live with her boyfriend. I had so many questions, but before I could speak, she told me I would take her place and assume her role in the organization. My eyes must have been the size of beach balls as she gave me the news.

The papers under her hands were a rough outline of her transition plan. Over the next hour, we walked through it together. We made adjustments, lining up the transition plan with her delivery date and the product delivery date. She listened to my concerns and challenged my doubts as we developed the business case for my title change and salary increase. We first needed to get to yes on the plan before asking for the title and dollars. As before, she pushed the red-lined papers to my side of the table and told me to put the pitch together. "We are meeting with leadership later today, and you will share the plan," she said.

Time was important because this news would travel fast in our small company. I think I might have skipped back to my cube to put the presentation together. A few short hours later, Caryn and I sat opposite a few key leaders in the boardroom. As I presented our plan, I could feel the blood rising to my face from nerves. After a ping-pong of questions and answers, the plan was generally accepted. Then, the final hurdle. It was the first time I had asked for a raise or a promotion, and certainly not in a group environment.

The leaders listened as I shakenly laid out my ask. There was general acknowledgment and recognition of the enormity of the role I was eager to take on. However, they wanted an opportunity to discuss and get back to me. As I left, I knew I had at least one advocate in the room that would no doubt be heard.

My plan and promotion were approved, but the salary request was granted based on a "proving" period. I received the title change and a partial salary bump, with the full salary increase four months after meeting some performance milestones largely focused on leadership. I did ultimately receive the full salary.

In that moment, I couldn't fully appreciate what Caryn had done for me. Superficially, she lined me up perfectly to step into her role. One could argue that it was dumb luck or good fortune that I fell into this situation, but Caryn was under no obligation to do any of it. She could have put up the electric fence around her work and mine and left me in my cube to focus on documentation. She also could have come in, given her notice, interviewed a replacement, and moved on. Instead, she helped me build my skills so that I had upward mobility. She put me in a few intense situations so that I was fire-tested. She taught me how to use my voice to ask. **Most importantly, she taught me to be swift and deliberate in acting opportunistically.**

That was exactly the help I needed.

Money is always a tricky topic, and asking for more money from your employer is universally recognized as a very uncomfortable activity. So much so that many employees choose to avoid the topic altogether and hope for the recognition they deserve when annual pay increases are considered. Despite some recent changes, salary information is not readily available in many industries, and pay increases don't follow any standard guidelines. A reluctance to talk about money amongst staff means that even the range of what's possible to ask for is anyone's guess. It's common to move jobs every 5-10 years, so get comfortable being uncomfortable with negotiating compensation.

The same applies to promotions. While most people are comfortable applying for a new position within their company or outside it when one is formally posted, they are often reluctant to seek out potential opportunities or make a case for being moved up when nothing concrete seems to be available. For many, the perceived "way things are done" within an organization can be enough to hold them back from being proactive in creating their own opportunities. The wait-and-see approach has never been my style, and I think it's the wrong approach in most business environments. It doesn't mean that timing isn't important. It's about understanding the needs of your company and the wider industry in which it operates and identifying the right time to create or seize an opportunity. **If you don't ask, the answer is always no.**

Risk

I believe the biggest risk for women regarding pay raises and promotions is waiting for opportunities rather than seeking out or creating them for themselves. My experience of being recognized by my manager and trained in advance to take over her position was incredible. It is also rare. Unless you are satisfied waiting for an annual pay raise cycle to come back around before receiving one or a formal job posting to pop up to apply for a promotion, you will have to be proactive about seeking out more money or better opportunities. You are responsible for navigating your career trajectory, and to succeed, you must tie what is best for you to what's best for the company in a way that is evident to the higher-ups. **If not you, then who?**

Building Confidence in Your Abilities

One of the most significant barriers women often face is the nagging presence of doubts and insecurities, from questioning one's competence and qualifications to fearing failure or not being taken seriously in a professional setting. To overcome these barriers, building confidence in your professional abilities is essential. **If you don't believe you are worth what you are asking for, neither will your boss!** Building professional self-confidence can include reframing negative self-talk and challenging limiting beliefs about what you can achieve. Competence is not synonymous with perfection, which is a way women often hold themselves back. Setbacks and mistakes are natural parts of the learning process. By embracing a growth mindset and viewing challenges as opportunities for learning and development, you can cultivate resilience and confidence in your abilities.

Improving self-confidence can also be achieved by investing in continuous learning and skill development. What skills or certifications does the competition likely have that you don't? I embarked on getting my PMP certification (project management professional) because that's what I needed if I were to apply for a job at another company. It's an exhausting application process in which you must prove your years of prior experience through meticulous documentation, learn the detailed framework, and then pass an exam to prove your capability as a project manager. So, even though it wasn't required for my role, people hired into similar roles after me at my company needed it, and I wanted to ensure I was meeting the revised qualifications.

I chose to get my RMP (risk management professional), a similarly exhaustive process, because I was assigned many rescue projects. These are initiatives that are $$$ over budget and months or years behind schedule, and I was being asked to lead them and make them successful. I got my RMP to help distinguish myself from all the PMPs doing similar project rescue work. It was a differentiator for me (and still is) and allowed me to talk about how I understood the dynamics and complexities of preventative performance.

In some cases, it's not skill development that needs to happen but rather skill recognition. In Chapter 3, we discussed creating a one-year plan for reaching certain career goals following a performance evaluation. Part of that plan involves creating short-term career advancement goals and understanding how to use the right language to increase visibility and recognition. Maybe you don't have the vision I had of standing in a corner office with a big window in a power suit overlooking an urban landscape. Still, whatever your vision is, you need a plan to either develop certain skills or to identify the skills you've already been building that you haven't realized you've been building. A great example is someone in a customer service role who has been answering phones or taking criticism from customers on a regular basis. They are cultivating MAD SKILLS that can translate into higher levels of employment where listening emphatically, remaining calm, and making quick decisions are essential skills.

If you have been taking your skills for granted or downplaying them because they don't feel as important as others, it's time to stop. Don't forget to include skills you develop in volunteer or non-work contexts that can translate to business. You are the sum of the sum of all your skills and experiences. Many people believe that successful people are just lucky—they are in the right place at the right time or have the right connections. While that may be true for a small number of people, that's not the case for most. I believe that "luck" is where preparation meets opportunity. You must prepare first so that you can be ready when the opportunity arises. What might that look like in practice?

If you're looking for a raise, make a list of all your skills and connect them to your current role in ways that support the company's objectives and success. Use direct language, and quantify your impact when possible.

If you're aiming for a promotion, use that same list to compare your skills against those required for the job you want and to show how they would be best used in the new role.

If you're having difficulty identifying your skills, ask a friend or trusted colleague for help or refer back to your most recent performance appraisal. List the work or different hats you've been wearing and then tie them to the skills required. You are building a framework for you—your secret sauce, if you will.

In my case, there are a lot of people who can manage projects. Millions of people have a PMP, so what is it about my skills that are unique or amazing? If you don't know the answer for yourself, ask a trusted source. In a performance review, one of my female managers once said, "One of Tiffany's strongest areas is her ability to wade through the weeds and gray areas and boil things down into a straightforward action plan. Getting stuck in the spin cycle can be extremely frustrating and too easy. Tiffany is the most effective in keeping things in perspective, keeping the teams focused on the right issues, and most importantly, keeping things moving forward." A light bulb went off for me. That's exactly what I bring to the table. That's my secret sauce.

Once you do the work to create your "luck," you'll be ready when an opportunity presents itself, and others will wonder how you got so lucky!

Embrace Growth Opportunities

It's easy to get good at what you do and stay in that lane longer than you should. It feels good to be the go-to expert, meet all your goals and objectives consistently, and have days when you feel you could do your job with your eyes closed. You must take chances on new opportunities by stepping out of your comfort zone and trying new things to move ahead. When my manager was preparing me to take over her role, she included me in meetings and presentations with some of our most difficult clients so that I could learn how to navigate those situations.

Would it have been easier for me to only take on those clients who were easy to deal with? Of course. But it wouldn't have prepared me to take over her role, and it certainly wouldn't have been enough for upper leadership to be convinced of my abilities to do so. I learned how to handle tough client meetings, criticism, and hard conversations *before* it was part of my job description, and that experience helped me secure the promotion. You may have to get creative and put yourself out there, so to speak, to get experience outside of your current niche.

If you are eyeing a promotion in a different department, consider seeking networking opportunities or mentorships with someone from that department. One trick I've learned along the way is to ask people in positions you want to be in or admire for a bit of their time. Send an email introducing yourself, and follow with something like, "I'm a [insert role] in department [insert department name], and I'm thinking about my career development. Would you have 20 to 30 minutes to speak with me about your path to [insert role]?"

Most people are flattered to get that kind of request (wouldn't you be?) and typically don't turn it down. So get 20-30 minutes of their time, and ask what key skills they have. Not only will you walk away with some key insights, but you have likely built an ally. It might feel awkward at first, but if you can't take the risk to ask someone to tell you about themselves, it will be a real struggle to take the risk to ask for a raise or promotion. Not to mention, you are practicing the hardest of all people skills to master—Listening! And you'll need this skill if/when you manage people.

Keep in mind that growth opportunities are not always work-related. Volunteer opportunities, participating in local associations or community organizations, networking, or participating in activities of interest to you not associated with your job can provide you with valuable skills that translate to your career. Coaching, Guiding or Scout leader, and working with vulnerable communities in hospitals or shelters all provide excellent skills transferable to the workplace. Volunteering for the PTA involves fundraising, event planning, negotiation, compromise, public speaking, and communication skills. Much of the community work that tends to be female-dominated requires higher-level skills that are much sought after in today's economy if you know how to communicate their value to your current or prospective employer.

About a dozen years ago, I reported indirectly to a VP. I was just starting out as a manager, building my team. I had a job opening, and I was reviewing resumes and beginning interviews. I received a woman's resume looking to re-enter the workforce after around a decade of being a stay-at-home mom. She didn't have any near-term or recent skills or technology requirements that the role needed, but she had done some really interesting things ten years prior before she had children and became a full-time mom.

While considering her resume, this VP had said to me that he would never turn down hiring a woman who had "managed the home and the kids" for as many years as she had because he believed that not only had she kept pace, but she probably outpaced interpersonal skill development and that should be strongly considered. He had a family of his own and had watched his wife manage the logistics of the family life. He strongly believed that the skills it took to do so were absolutely able to be translated into the project management role on my team. This candidate managed school events, fundraisers, club sports teams, and the different personalities that come with those organizations, kept the house schedule, and figured out the family logistics. My VP was very clearly able to translate what she was doing at home into business terms, such as schedule management, logistics, people management, and more. He displayed strong male allyship (before such a term existed) in recognizing that it would benefit the business to bring a woman with strong skills back into the workforce. I hired her, and she was a great addition to the team. I ended up learning a lot from her as I grew my skills as a manager.

Asking for a Raise

Negotiating a pay raise is a crucial aspect of career advancement, yet it's a conversation that many individuals approach with trepidation. While initial salary negotiations set the foundation for compensation, renegotiating for a raise requires a different approach that underscores your value, accomplishments, and continued growth within the organization. Building upon the strategies outlined for salary negotiations, it's essential to highlight your ongoing contributions, expanded responsibilities, and any additional skills or qualifications acquired since your last salary discussion. Despite the stereotype that women are more uncomfortable than men asking for raises, in 2022, men and women asked for raises at the same rate, 11%.

Unfortunately, women are less likely to receive that raise, at 52% for women vs. 59% for men. The consequences for women are huge. "As a result of the gender pay gap, a woman who begins a full-time career today stands to miss out on $417,400 over the course of a 40-year career." And that is just salary! When you add in bonuses and other financial incentives tied to base salary, the gap widens. While those numbers can be depressing, I see them as fuel for encouraging women to ask for what they deserve in a way that is more likely to get a yes. While transparency laws can help improve the wage gap by up to 50%, it is not something women can rely on to get them the pay they have earned by being high performers, particularly in industries that don't employ transparency models. **It's up to you to advocate for what you deserve.**

When preparing for a renegotiation, gather examples of your achievements and impact within the organization, such as exceeding targets, successful projects, or positive feedback from clients or colleagues, and build a compelling case for why you deserve a pay raise. Begin with your most recent accomplishments over the last six months, and then include the most relevant accomplishments from the last year or any ongoing long-term projects. Provide statistics and connect the benefits to the company's bottom line when possible. Emphasize your value proposition and the tangible benefits you bring to the company in your role.

While it is helpful to research industry standards and market trends to ensure your salary expectations are realistic and competitive, it is more important that you know where your salary falls on the company's salary scale for the role. Research industry ranges, considering location, as pay rates can vary greatly. Pay raises range from 3% to 5% on average, but several factors can justify a higher rate. How long has it been since your last raise? Have your job duties significantly changed? What other benefits are you receiving (or not)? Based on your research, are you earning significantly less than the industry standard?

If you have been in a company for a while or your job has significantly changed, you can always work with your manager and HR and ask for a compensation audit for your role. In a case like this, the justification could be the number of years you have been in your role vs. a new or similar role that has opened up. For example, if you were hired five years ago at $50k and have gotten steady increases to your base, how does it compare with the salary of a new hire with the same skills that you had five years ago? In most cases, it is higher than what you are being paid now. This justifies an adjustment so you can be adequately compensated for the five years of experience over the new hire.

Before entering into renegotiations, go back to the mutual gains theory of negotiation and prepare for the meeting. What bridge is too big for you to cross? What are you willing to compromise, knowing that the goal is for both parties to walk away satisfied with the outcome? During the renegotiation conversation, approach the discussion confidently and professionally, clearly articulating your accomplishments, aspirations, and desired compensation. Be prepared to negotiate and compromise if necessary, but also know your worth and be willing to advocate for fair compensation. Maintain open communication and a collaborative mindset throughout the process. Everyone likes a "good deal."

Consider how you would respond to objections. If you are doing a good job today for $20 an hour, why would your boss pay you more to do the same job? One possible reason is knowing how much time and money it would cost them to interview, hire, and train someone else. Nine out of ten times, it will cost the company more, not only in money but also in time to do that. It's helpful to think about possible objections in advance and role-play to get comfortable with countering a no. You can even role-play with AI tools to help you become more confident. Using this example, if your manager can avoid the inconvenience of reviewing resumes, interviewing, and training someone new for even $10 more per hour, giving you a raise could actually be a deal!

Finally, present your request in writing as well. Your direct manager is often not the person who makes the final decision, so having your ask and justification for it clearly laid out in writing can help. Your manager is unlikely to remember all the details of your accomplishments when relaying your request, so having a written summary can ensure that all the relevant information is passed on exactly as you want it to be received.

Consider it a partnership with your manager and HR. Depending on your manager's personality, you may or may not want to come into the meeting with ALL your cards on the table, but you should have them ready. In my example with Steve, he was eager to help me achieve something. We partnered on the documentation, and then I let him carry it forward to HR. It goes back to the concept of a win-win. Steve got the chance to develop skills in a team member and then advocate for them in front of leadership, all things that were likely performance indicators for his next review!

Rejection

Navigating disappointment and rejection in career advancement is a challenging yet inevitable aspect of professional growth. The emotional toll can be significant, whether it's not getting the role you applied for, not receiving the raise you anticipated, or facing rejection in job applications. It can evoke many emotions, including frustration, self-doubt, and inadequacy. It's crucial to allow yourself the space to process these feelings without judgment, acknowledging that setbacks are an inherent part of striving for success. I like to use "no" to fuel my next pitch.

Separating No from Not Yet

When is a no not really a no?

Sometimes, the response we get to an ask isn't what we want to hear. At that moment, it can be difficult to tell the difference between a hard "no" and a more subtle "not yet." So, if not now, then when?

When Steve told me that raises weren't typically granted out of the regular cycle, he wasn't telling me I wasn't worthy of a raise or would not be receiving one; he was telling me, "Not yet." You may be passed over for a promotion and given feedback on improving your chances for next time, turning what feels like a no into a not yet. When I was approved to take over Caryn's role, I also negotiated a salary increase to reflect the increased responsibilities of the job. Except I didn't receive all of it immediately. The amount I requested was approved based on certain conditions being met following a "proving period," as described earlier in the chapter. I received a "not yet" despite the increase being approved in theory. In many cases, a rejection feels like an outright no when it is really *not yet*.

Figuring out which one is which can be tough. If I had met all the proving period requirements and leadership pushed back with more requirements before giving me my raise, I would have realized that the not yet was actually a no, and I was being strung along. When that happens, you must make a tough decision about your future with the company. While you can't always be certain that a not yet will turn into a yes, as promised, there are steps you can take to minimize the chances of that happening.

1- **Get specific.** What are the conditions under which a not yet will be turned into a yes? If management doesn't know exactly what would lead to a yes, chances are it's actually a no.

   For me, it was tied to product development milestones. I had to have 100% of the KNOWN product scope documented as user stories based on the current KNOWN requirements in line with the timeline for development and testing for 1.0 go-live, although there was some wiggle room if the scope changed. I also needed to be the subject matter expert (SME) for the

Sales organization and was tasked with presenting the 1.0 product at the largest industry conference of the year.

2- **Have a timeframe.** You don't want to be left hanging forever. It's up to you what amount of time is acceptable to wait before something changes, but I suggest thinking in months, not a year or more. My proving period was four months, coinciding with a product launch commitment to the board of directors. Consider the requirements you've been given, and if your supervisor hasn't put a specific timeline on them, decide on one yourself. Perhaps you will exceed certain targets for the next three months and then approach them again for the full salary to be delivered. Have a timeframe and stick to it. Also, make it a short timeframe.

3- **Get it in writing.** Whether completing a course, reaching a sales goal, or receiving a certain level on a performance review, ask for the terms and conditions in writing. This helps avoid any confusion or misunderstandings and gives you an idea of whether your company is serious about turning a not yet into a yes or not. A partnership with your manager and HR is beneficial. Your manager may have the best intentions, but it may not come to fruition if human resources doesn't support it. Many big companies use the goals documented in your last performance review to measure against in your next one, so if your goals change mid-year, talk to HR and see if you can adjust them.

4- **Meet the requirements.** I received my raise because I met the requirements of my proving period. If you have been given parameters within your control to get what you have asked for, ensure you put your energy into meeting them within the set timeline.

You may do everything right only to realize that the not yet was always a no. In this case, I recommend you prepare a backup plan. Is it worth staying in the company for the wider opportunities that may be available to you or because your personal circumstances don't support a move at this time? Or is it time to go? A backup plan before you hit the deadline can help mitigate disappointment and avoid making big decisions under less-than-ideal circumstances.

Resilience

When it comes to being resilient after missing out on a pay raise or promotion, there is a fine line between exhibiting resilience, preparing for the next opportunity, and putting up with being overlooked and undervalued. It is a distinction only you can make, but you must be aware of the difference.

Many career guides or mentors encourage the "take on more responsibility without title or pay" approach to show you are capable. That is one way to handle rejection, but it must come with a documented salary or promotion catch-up plan.

I give people too much credit that they will be fair, and they aren't. If the specifics are not agreed upon upfront, too many things can happen (i.e., company downturn) that change the landscape and "understanding." As Ronald Regan said, "Trust, but verify." I trust that people want to be fair, but I need to have a way to be sure that what they are promising can be vetted in some way. Most HR personnel want to retain good employees, so partner with them to find an acceptable solution.

Take the time between opportunities to review your career plan, make changes accordingly, and don't stop looking for new opportunities. Perhaps you are waiting for a new pay raise review in six months, but a promotion opportunity pops up that would pay you even more than the raise. If you think it's the right fit, go for it! Much like most things in life, progress isn't linear. The career trajectory you have mapped out will most likely not go exactly according to plan.

Reset

Sometimes, rejection or missing out on one opportunity is a sign to reset our priorities. If you have been turned down for a raise or promotion more than once, or despite presenting overwhelming justification for why you deserve more compensation, consider reassessing your career goals and aspirations. Consider what motivates you and where your passions lie, and use it to chart a new course forward.

Identify the lessons learned from past experiences and incorporate these insights into your new goals to ensure they are realistic and meaningful. Once you've identified your new goals, develop a strategic plan for advancement. Actively seek out new opportunities that align with your revised goals and aspirations. It may involve networking with professionals in your field, attending industry events or conferences, or exploring job openings within your organization or beyond. Be open to new challenges and stepping outside your comfort zone to broaden your horizons and expand your skill set.

Networking is a powerful tool for career advancement, especially after experiencing setbacks. Cultivate relationships with professionals in your industry or field of interest, both online and offline. Engage in meaningful conversations, offer support and assistance to others, and be proactive in seeking mentorship or guidance. Networking can open doors to new opportunities and provide valuable insights and advice as you pursue your goals. The saying, *It's not what you know, it's who you know* is true!

Finally, know when it's time to go. If your efforts and accomplishments are not adequately recognized or rewarded, it's time to seek opportunities elsewhere. A rejection can be a wake-up call for the better. I've been there.

I worked for a small but mighty software company along the way. They were a wholly owned subsidiary of a much larger company. The software company operated independently for many years, with its own colors, logos, culture, and benefits, completely separate from the parent company. Once we became profitable and successful, the larger company absorbed us into their organization as a revenue-generating line of business. And the entire landscape changed; it became more rigid.

The parent company brought in a new CEO, with the philosophy that there should be no more than eight layers between him at the top of the organization and the employees at the bottom, in a company of approximately 10,000 employees. As a result, we underwent a massive reorganization. Part of that reorganization meant removing all the "senior" and "associate" titles, such as Senior Director or Associate Manager. The positions became Director or Manager. On a practical level, for employees, it meant that many jobs were being eliminated or amalgamated. Suddenly, people had to reapply for their jobs, competing against 30 or 40 others who were also trying to hold onto their positions amid the downsizing.

I was a senior manager on the doorstep for a director role. Instead of reapplying for a manager position, I was applying for all the director jobs. The competition within my own company was intense for director positions, and I wasn't successful in getting one. However, I was offered a manager position identical to the one I had, which meant I survived the company reorganization. Not everyone on my team survived. It was my job to lay them off.

During that time, I felt like I was constantly delivering bad news. We were changing benefits, salary structures, reporting structures, expense, and reimbursement policies. You name it, and I likely had to deliver bad news about it. It was gut-wrenching for everyone. After personally having invested so much in building a high-performing team with amazing rapport and the results to prove it, I was disassembling it. The hardest thing I've had to do in my career to date.

Despite the long days and hard conversations, it gave me time to reevaluate what I wanted to do in my career and if it was still the company for me. Within 9 to 12 months of the reorganization and everything shaking out, I realized, "This doesn't feel good. It's no longer where I want to be." I began looking for another job. Using all the information I had gathered about my role, my results, and my impact, I began a job search. Eventually, I could walk away from the company on my own terms.

Chapter Summary

- Understand the needs of your company and the wider industry in which it operates, and identify the right time to create or seize an opportunity.

- Improve your self-confidence by recognizing the skills you do have and building the ones you need to move forward professionally.

- Seek out opportunities for growth that will serve you both in your current position and improve your chances of getting the position you want.

- When negotiating from a "not yet" to a yes, get the conditions in writing. If you meet those conditions and are not given the raise or promotion promised, it may be time to move on.

- Provide your own requests in writing, outlining not only the specifics of your ask but also your justification behind it.

- Know when you are being overlooked or taken for granted, and be proactive in looking elsewhere for new opportunities where your talents will be rewarded accordingly.

Chapter 5

From Crisis to Confidence: Navigating Layoffs and Embracing Change for Growth

I've been laid off twice in my career.

The first time was early, in my first job out of college (The job from Chapter 1, where the VP, Matt, whom I had caddied for, had hired me as a pricing analyst right after graduation.) The company had two lines of business focused on engineering and technical staffing; one in commercial and light manufacturing and the other in military government contracting. They occupied a two-story building that physically separated the two divisions. The commercial division and business operations were located on the 1st floor. The government contracting team, c-suite, and legal occupied the top floor. I worked on the top floor with the government contracting team, tracking performance against the current government contracts, monitoring prospective opportunities coming up for bids, and managing the pricing proposals for new bids. There were different vibes between the two floors. The top floor had more open space, bigger working cubes, offices, and meeting rooms, and the library was also quiet. A loud laugh would carry through the whole floor. The 1st floor had the bustle of an airport—the buzz of people coming and going, crowded areas everywhere, chatter, and few places to find quiet.

I enjoyed my first "real job." I enjoyed the challenge it presented around organization and tracking. The volume of numbers and formulas running through tabbed workbooks tested my attention to detail. The company had generously invested in me not only through that master's degree but also by sending me to DC and other military bases to learn the business and the business of government contracting. My awareness of outside impacts on an industry was also new. Sure, I had learned about the outside forces in business school, but it's different to experience it. The revenue strength of this company was military-focused government contracts. In the late 1990s, Bill Clinton was in his 2nd term as the President of the United States. The country was stable, and there were limited conflicts globally, so the need for military contracting was declining, and the rules around government contracting were changing. Not only were there fewer opportunities to bid, but the bids were now more competitive than ever before. In my first 12 months with the company, we simply didn't win many new contracts.

At that time, my VP started talking to me about building skills for another part of the business for another leader. I was open to it. I wasn't particularly busy in my pricing analyst role and have always been open to new learning. I'd moonlight as a technical recruiter downstairs, on the 1st floor. The new role required a lot of people skills and persuasion. I wasn't specifically responsible for selling services into a new account; I was responsible for maintaining it by placing quality people in the account. That role came with an opportunity to earn more money based on commission and to work in a faster-paced, competitive division. The VP of that division, Tom, was a good guy. He knew he needed to build my skills, was genuinely interested in coaching a newbie, and gave me opportunities to succeed and fail. Not more than a month later, my shared role between the 1st floor and the 2nd floor became a full-time role on the 1st floor.

A few months later, I was asked to take the lead on a new account, but there was a catch (isn't there always). I had to be onsite at the new account from 5 am - 2 pm every workday to manage our on-site contractors. It was a solid 60-minute driving commute each way, AND I was only halfway through my master's degree program, taking night courses. So, of course, I said yes. For the next six months or so, it was early to bed and early to rise to manage this account. Except, of course, for those three nights a week in which I had night school, then it was early to rise, drive west to work, drive east to school, nap (if possible), class, and drive back home right to bed. I did get comp time off to study and take exams, but it was as exhausting as it sounds. I kept this schedule most of the time I was going through the master's program. I did it largely independently without much help from the main office. Of course, if I needed help, I called or emailed the main office. But I wasn't going to the main office, and they weren't coming to me either. One Friday, I was asked to come to the main office for some meetings rather than go to the customer site. I didn't question it. It meant I could sleep in (till 7 am) the day after a night class. Yay!

When I arrived, a coworker, Don, a retired marine, greeted me at the door. He was always the first one to the office. The doors didn't open until 8:30 am, so if you were early, Don would have to manually unlock it for you and lock it behind you again. His job was to turn on the lights, start the coffee maker, and lock/unlock the doors. On this particular morning, he opened the door for me and escorted me upstairs to Matt's office. Highly unusual. Matt and Tom were both there, which was unusual. We all sat down on the dark brown leather couches. The couch was cold but more comfortable than the conversation we were about to have. On the coffee table was a green file folder with my termination letter and severance offer.

I don't remember the words that were spoken, only the feelings. *Shock.* I was completely caught by surprise. I never saw it coming. Not even a remote possibility. *Tears.* I'm sure it was ugly. As a successful athlete, I had never been cut from anything before in my life, and here I was being cut from a job! It was a gut punch. *Betrayal.* I thought I had a friendship with Matt that we had built over the years. Why didn't he protect me? Warn me?

It was hard to comprehend, and it happened quickly. Before I knew it, Don escorted me back out of the building and to my car. I was a complete mess driving home that day. I couldn't stop thinking about all the bills I had to pay, and I now had no job. *Fear.* I had no financial plan to cover a significant unemployment gap. *Shame.* It showed up when I called my husband and had to say the words out loud, and every time after that, I had to tell someone else I didn't have a job.

I was utterly unprepared for that day, emotionally, financially, or otherwise. It took a few days, but the big emotions passed, and I was able to re-read and consider the company's offer. I received a severance package, which was a two-week salary pay. The company policy was to pay one week of salary and benefits for every year employed with the organization. With some coaching from a family member, I negotiated slightly better terms, which helped temporarily ease the financial burden. But no amount of compensation could make any of the other feelings go away.

The cluelessness, the complete surprise, was the one that lasted the longest. I went into game analysis mode—I analyzed the whole situation many times over, trying to figure out what I missed, how I missed it, and what I was NOT going to miss again:

1- **Paying attention to the business landscape.** Continued revenue loss or loss of potential revenue opportunities are not sustainable. In this situation, I didn't recognize how critical the one line of business was to the company's overall success, and the true impact of losing those bids was felt organization-wide.

2- **Shifting of resources or reporting structure changes.** Most managers want to retain talent where they can, and shifting resources to other departments is a way they can temporarily win at balancing a budget shortfall and retaining already invested talent.

3- **Being out of sight is being out of mind.** I don't believe spending more time in the main office and less time at the client site would have changed my outcome. The skills I gained on-site working alongside the Client's team added real value to my resume. However, not having a regular presence in front of your leadership and not sharing your wins or challenges directly with them leaves you vulnerable and dependent on others communicating on your behalf. Very few people will deliver your message as well and you can, so be mindful that you are also championing your own story regularly.

Just over 15 years later, I was laid off for the second time. This one, I saw coming. I had much more work experience, better business awareness, and, with some experience on the management side laying off team members, a new perspective. As a result, I was better prepared for it on the back end of things.

In the second layoff, the executive leader who originally hired me and championed my growth at the company, Dave, was replaced suddenly. The woman who replaced him was excellent, and we developed a wonderful relationship that still exists. However, I didn't report to her. I had been moved to report to a manager in a different city with a dotted line report to a different executive leader in a third city. My role hadn't changed; I was still being asked to help develop business opportunities in a new local industry niche, but the expected timeline did change.

Under Dave, we had a plan. We set some targets and small goals. We agreed that these new market opportunities would take a few years and hard work to develop relationships with key leaders, but as long as we (and by "we," I mean ME) kept hitting those small goals, we'd get there. The change in leadership ushered in a change in expectations, as it usually does. They had new expectations for evolving that line of business in a far shorter period, less than a year. These conversations went on for some months. Leadership's expectations for how quickly I was expected to develop that new market didn't match my own expectations.

Ultimately, the company decided they couldn't tolerate the length of time it would take for that role to have an impact and that their original expectation wouldn't work. My new leadership informed me that they were abandoning that market pursuit and asked that I move into a different part of the business. It was a role that I wasn't interested in. I didn't think it was a good fit for my skills, it didn't align with my career goals, and it required a bigger sacrifice for my family. So, we were at an impasse.

When I declined the role, I suspected a larger reduction in force was looming, and I would be putting my name on that list. Doing so allowed me to have some control over that exit package, making the overall situation much less stressful. The decision didn't blindside me, and I was in a better place emotionally and financially. That layoff situation was empowering for me. Yes, ending up on the cut list is never good, but this time it stung less. The company made a decision that wasn't about me, and I made a decision that was! This turned out to be one of the best things that ever happened because I created my own company after leaving this job, which is a completely different book.

Management Perspective on Layoffs

If you work long enough or move up high enough in a company, there's a chance that you may one day be on the other side of the table during the layoff process, which also brings with it the chance to reflect and perhaps decide that it's time to change the course of your own career path. Between my first layoff in the early 2000s and my second in 2016, I had some full-circle moments as a manager where I had to lay off some of my team members. Remember the VP who encouraged me to hire the stay-at-home mom? He came through for me again by preparing me to have that termination conversation and deliver that severance notice. Of course, it is more difficult to be the person who is let go, but it can be extremely difficult and emotional for the manager who must relay the news.

In that instance, I wasn't involved in the decision-making around how the company would decide who would be laid off. I was invited to one meeting in which upper management informed me of the decision and the timing, which does not always happen. Decisions are typically made much, much higher up than the manager level and then simply passed along without any type of consultation or input.

I remember not getting any sleep the night before. My team member being laid off was a wonderful man with a family, someone I had gotten to know personally during our time working together, and in the morning, I was going to tell him he no longer had a job. I was on the West Coast, and the VP and the employee were in different cities in Eastern Standard Time, so the notification needed to be done over the phone (video calls were not prevalent) and early in the workday. I had a phone call with the company's VP at 4:30 a.m. so he could walk me through the process in advance. He explained that we would keep it simple and short and emailed me a script of three or four sentences. He was kind enough to ask me if I had ever done it before, and when I said no, he offered to take the lead on it, to which I agreed.

He explained the legalities around what we could and could not say and was clear that we were to stick to the script as closely as possible. This person was an experienced employee who had been through downsizing before, so we did not expect a negative reaction. Still, the VP shared what he and I would do IF things *did* get negative. We then called the employee together. The call lasted seven or eight minutes, which in some ways felt like the longest of my life but, at the same time, the shortest as well. It took less than ten minutes to change someone's life. We stuck to the script and went from there.

As I moved up in leadership, I became more involved in decision-making. This is where everything I have been discussing in this book comes together in choosing who to keep and who to let go. I look at performance reviews, growth potential, and skills that may be transferable to other organizational positions or departments. Most managers try to go through all the different options. Maybe not every manager or every company, but most managers want to retain talent where they can. Still, some financial decisions just can't be reconciled. The fact that the company did not bring in enough revenue to keep you isn't necessarily a reflection on you or your work.

That's the help I needed.

Risk

In the world of business, layoffs are inevitable. Businesses change, the economy goes through recessions, mergers and takeovers cause redundancies—a million factors can cause a business to lay off employees. Does it mean that every employee will be laid off in their lifetime? Of course not. That doesn't mean you shouldn't be prepared for the possibility.

In my opinion, the risk isn't the layoff. It lies in the pre–and post-layoff period.

Be Prepared Before You're Laid Off

I wasn't prepared to be laid off the first time it happened. At all. Looking back now, the signs were all there, but I was in my first post-college job and didn't know what I didn't know. I didn't have a contingency plan or a network. I got through it, but it was tougher than needed. I don't want that to happen to you. Getting laid off is hard enough in the best of circumstances. Being prepared can take some of the fear and uncertainty away.

Everyone's situation is different, but some things can help most people prepare for unexpected job loss.

1- **Keep your resume and skills profile up-to-date:** If you've been following along from the beginning, you can probably guess what I'm going to say here. If you need to look for another job on short notice, it's much easier if you aren't scrambling to get your professional story in order. Keep your resume updated using the type of language discussed in earlier chapters that articulates your value to the organization. Keep your professional social media profiles updated as well.

2- **Build a network inside the company:** Layoffs can sometimes be avoided if you can be placed elsewhere in the company. However, you won't be the only person trying to find another place where you fit. Taking the time to get to know employees in other divisions before a crisis can position you to be at the top of someone's mind if the time comes. It can also be useful for upward mobility within the company at any point.

3- **Build a network outside the company:** You don't have to join every professional association or committee to build a network outside your current job, but making some effort is worthwhile. If you are let go completely from the company, having a list of even just five people to connect with in your search for a new job can get the professional ball rolling. Also, networking can give you insights into moves happening within the industry in general. Informal rumors often swirl about company changes long before anything is formally announced. If you are paying attention, you might get a hint of what's coming in advance.

4- **Prepare financially:** We can't all have huge emergency funds and no debt, but knowing that you can stay afloat for a few months can give you the breathing room you need to figure out what's next.

How to Handle the Immediate Post-Layoff Period

The first month following a layoff is pivotal for getting yourself back in the game. It can be disorienting and difficult to know what to do first, so I've created a four-week plan to help you deal with the loss and prepare for the future.

Week 1: Do nothing work-related (if possible). Binge-watch something, do something in the middle of the day you normally would have missed, drive the school/sports carpool, or have lunch with that friend you keep saying "we should do lunch" with. Give yourself a few days before figuring it all out. Then, prepare to review the paperwork and know the "due date."

Week 2: Review the termination paperwork, consider your options, and consult a lawyer if needed. Before doing anything else or making any decisions, double-check the laws in your state. It's not unusual for an acceptance period on the severance offer or to include a non-disclosure agreement. If you need more clarification or are pressured to take action you are uncomfortable with, seek legal advice or contact your state's unemployment office. Many employment lawyers will offer a free consultation specifically for these situations. In the meantime, start updating your profile or resume.

Week 3: If you get laid off unexpectedly and didn't have the chance to reach out to people before the layoff, take the initiative to reach out as soon as you can after it. Many people will be looking for jobs, so getting your name front and center is key. Even if you aren't looking to immediately jump into a new role, reconnecting with contacts can give you valuable information about potential projects that may be of interest. Schedule a few calls with people in your network, including your mentors and your champions. Even if you haven't spoken to them in months, let them build your confidence, remind you of how awesome you are, and give you ideas and suggestions on where to look next. Let them be inputs to re-assessing your career plan.

Week 4: Take your first REAL steps to find your next opportunity, whether it's job searching, applying, or networking. It will likely take you a few weeks to find your confidence and your footing, so take that time. Maybe, like me, the layoff is the nudge you need to change the path you were on entirely. What better time than during a forced work hiatus to make sure the vision you thought you had for your career still suits you?

Beyond Week 4: Take imperfect action and Fail Fast. Keep reaching out to your network and try new things. It doesn't need to be perfect; it simply needs to keep the forward momentum going.

Rejection

I want to go back to my second layoff again because there are some important points I want to highlight, starting with dispelling the myth that it is always the least experienced or most recent hire who gets let go. That simply isn't true. By the time I was laid off for a second time, I had a solid decade of growth at the managerial level. All along, I had been following the same plan that I've been discussing in this book to chart my career path, including documenting my progress, quantifying my value to the organization, knowing what my strongest skills were, and, most importantly, knowing where I did and did not want my career to go, which is what led to the second layoff.

The company had unrealistic expectations for how quickly that role could evolve, which didn't match my expectations for how quickly I could evolve it or how long the market could take to evolve. I believed I would be set up for failure. Then, they wanted to place me in a role that I was not interested in. In the end, they decided that they couldn't tolerate the length of time it would take for that role to have an impact and that their original expectation wasn't going to work. When I talk about tolerance, I am referring to the financial tolerance of waiting for me to be able to make that role profitable for the company. It wasn't anything I specifically did, but it was more of an "Aha!" moment on their end. It's going to take us three years to make this division profitable? We don't have three years; we've only got one. Once they had that realization, they changed course and decided to shut down that particular line of business altogether.

In that time and in that organization, I had done all the things that we've talked about in this book, right? I built strong relationships and allies with other parts of the company. There were other people in the organization that I trusted. I could go to them and say, "Hey, they're thinking about closing my position. I'm going to be looking for some work. I need to move somewhere else in the company." I asked around for other opportunities and used that internal network to have those conversations. In the end, there wasn't anything suitable for me to move or transition to.

Knowing this, I was able to go back to the negotiating table and address the situation matter-of-factly. I said, "Where you want me to go is not where I want to go. It's not where I see my career going." From there, I was able to have some control over my exit, and we had an amicable split. The truth is that it still felt bad, but it was better than the first layoff. By seeing the signs and preparing in advance, I was able to have a softer landing. That is the best we can hope for in these scenarios.

Resilience

Losing a job, whether via layoff or being summarily fired, requires a different kind of resilience and mental toughness than not getting hired in the first place or being passed up for a pay raise. When you are not able to achieve something you want, such as a promotion, it can be seen through the lens of a temporary loss. You can try again for that raise, that promotion, that title. You can create a plan to reach that goal on the next try.

Being let go from a job involves mourning the loss of something you had attained and then lost. Staying resilient in the face of that can be more difficult. Despite understanding rationally that issues outside of your control contributed to the decision to let you go, there will always be an element of "Why me?" You may question what you could have done differently or why you were let go but not your colleague. You may feel betrayed by work relationships that you thought should have protected you or given you a warning. Or it can feel like rejection on a personal level, as if you had failed. Staying resilient and believing that something better will come along can be hard. Reach out to your support network of family and friends and take some time to regroup.

Reset

Take stock of where you are in your career plan, and decide on the next best step for you, whether it's a temporary or more long-term one. Then, dust yourself off and start putting that plan in motion. I looked for a new job following my first layoff. I started a company after my second. There's no one right answer for what a reset means for you. My advice is to embrace the possibilities and dream big. It's easy to get caught up in the day-to-day routine and responsibilities of a full-time job and push our dreams to the side. Now is your chance to give them the attention they deserve. That's a gift, even if it takes some time to see it.

Layoffs are hard and often inevitable, so don't let yourself dwell on it for too long before taking back control of your career and your future.

Chapter Summary

- Layoffs can happen to anyone at any stage in their career. It's best to be prepared.

- Learn to see the signs that big changes may be coming. A merger, a financial downturn, or a new CEO can signal changes that could lead to layoffs.

- Prepare in advance. Keep your resume updated, try to build an emergency fund, and have a backup plan in case of job loss.

- After a layoff, reach out to your network to inform people of your new status and to keep abreast of any potential opportunities.

- Take the time to reassess what you want from your career, and don't be afraid to change course if your goals have changed.

Chapter 6

The Job Search Journey: Strategies for Confidence, Clarity, and Showcasing Your Worth

Around the time I was getting married, my soon-to-be husband was laid off from a small company that struggled to make payroll each week. I was gainfully employed for an established BIG company that I could have grown with if I wasn't completely bored in my role and impatient with the pace. The economy wasn't great, and given the timing, one of us was likely to start our married life unemployed. We had two choices: 1- stay put and, if money got tight, go live with my parents OR 2- accept a job offer in another city. While I'm sure that it's every parent's dream to have their newly married daughter and son-in-law living in their basement, it wasn't ours. So, I resigned from my position at the boring BIG company and my fiancé took the job offer on the East Coast.

Moving, wedding events, and settling into a new house kept me busy for a few months. In the meantime, I submitted endless resumes to website blackholes. For some reason, I wasn't getting the traction I needed to land a position. At that time, recruitment was entering the age of recruiting databases. You emailed your resume to a generic email address, which was then picked up on the other side by a data entry person, not a hiring manager. The data entry person would enter your resume into a database that allowed keywords to be searched across hundreds of resumes. Incredibly efficient for the HR teams and recruiters, but not so great for applicants. This is not unlike the current challenges we are seeing with AI tools being used in both job searching and resume reviewing.

Frustrated with the process, I woke up one day with a new-old plan, determined to beat the system. I got in my car and drove to some of the office complexes around our new house. I then sat in the parking lot or walked into the lobby, writing down each company's name (no, the internet couldn't tell me this yet). I then returned home to research each company on the internet by guessing their web addresses (again, early-era internet). I learned that a half-dozen had open positions in a vertical in which I believed I had relevant or transferable skills. Not all of these companies had open positions that I would apply for, but the fact that they were hiring in the market at the time was a positive sign.

I printed some resumes on thick, luxurious paper. The kind of paper you notice before you toss it aside. I got dressed in my favorite pantsuit (navy blue with a baby pink camisole), and I drove back to the offices of those same companies. This time, I went into each one, attempting to speak with someone in Human Resources. In one office, a gentleman walked by as I was handing my resume to the receptionist and explaining my story. He worked in HR. He asked me a few questions, thanked me, and I was on my way. Not long after that, I got a call from that same company to come back in for a series of interviews. My new-old plan had worked. After a day of interviews, I received an offer and soon had a job!

What I didn't know until sometime later was that the woman who eventually hired me, Caryn, had been lingering in the coffee room adjacent to reception when I came in to deliver my resume. She intercepted my resume from the HR person, looked it over, and told him to call me back into the office. From her perspective, anyone willing to walk in a resume was clearly a self-starter who was motivated to work, two qualities she needed in someone responsible for driving out product requirements in a fledgling software company. You might remember Caryn from Chapter 4. She was instrumental in helping me move up in the company by training me to take over her role.

Looking back, I've found some interesting job opportunities in unorthodox ways. I was once randomly assigned to carry the golf bag for a member and his guest one hot day. It turned out that the guest was moving to the area to take on a CEO position for a large real estate company. We got to talking, and by the end of the round, he had offered me an internship in his marketing department. The next week, I interviewed with his VP of Marketing (the only female on his leadership team) and started shortly after that. My experiences highlight the truth that finding a job and moving up in a company often doesn't look like how we've been conditioned to think it does. And it could be holding you back.

That's why this chapter isn't going to be all about the "right way" to navigate the job search or how to tailor your resume *just so* because that isn't the help you need. Instead, I will help you navigate a path to job success that includes leveraging your personal and professional networks, aiming higher than you've been conditioned to do, and taking the right types of risks to increase your chances of success.

Risk

Not All Interviews Are Great

Two of my most memorable interviews happened at the same company. In the first interview, one of the interviewers decided to challenge me on the spelling of a particular software program that I had listed on my resume. He explained that he was a former English major and knew the spelling was wrong. As the current head of marketing, he was a peer to the hiring manager and part of the interview team. He took my resume, circled the name of a software program a few times, and handed it to me. He said, "Normally, I dismiss candidates that have misspellings on the resume." I had to fight the urge to correct HIM. While it's entirely possible that I did have a mistake on my resume, I remember being very meticulous about the spelling and formatting; that luxurious paper was expensive for someone who didn't have a job! I had specifically double-checked the spelling of the software program on the box (yes, software once came in boxes, off a shelf, at a store) before adding it to my resume, but he was convinced I had been careless.

He then made much of the rest of my interview about being diligent, fact-checking, and double-checking before turning things in at work. He was extremely condescending, talking down to me the entire interview, which was as awkward as it was annoying. Still, I knew that I wouldn't be working for or reporting to him, so I sat there nodding my head, making non-committal noises periodically, and then dismissed the incident. When I learned that despite my perceived inability to spell things correctly, I had moved on in the interview process, I was looking forward to the next round.

During the second round of interviews, they told me that I would need to take the equivalent of a typing test. TYPING. At this point in my career, I had a master's degree with a double emphasis in data mining and warehousing. I could write complex code and was being asked instead to prove that I knew how to use word processors, spreadsheets, and whatever other programs that were part of Office Suite. It was beyond insulting and even though I was unemployed, a waste of my time. I figured if the real decision for the position rested on whether or not I could, in fact, use Microsoft Office and Excel after having been in the workforce for nearly five years and having a technical degree, then it wasn't at the right level, and I certainly wasn't going to be using the skill set I wanted to be using. So when the HR person called to set it up, I politely declined a third trip to their offices.

She asked why. I explained that my skills in using those programs should be self-evident in both my academic and professional accomplishments. She told me that the hiring team had been burned in the past and wanted to be absolutely sure. When I declined again, she reminded me about how hard the job market was and how I shouldn't be so choosy and gave me a backhanded "good luck."

Yes, I took the risk to walk away as a result of the interview process. If the company was making me prove basic computer skill competency far below my skill, experience, and education level, then they had the wrong candidate, and I had the wrong job opportunity. Another indicator that shouldn't be overlooked was the way in which two people treated me during the interviewing process. When there's one negative interaction, it's easy to consider it an anomaly; you caught them on a bad day. However, when I had two interactions with different people on different days, offering me career advice in a patronizing tone, I felt it was an indicator of something more. A cultural norm in that company that wasn't likely to change because I proved I could manipulate a spreadsheet. I trusted my gut, kept applying for jobs, and eventually got that amazing opportunity to work for Caryn.

Two key points came out of these interviews for me.

1- **The interview process is not a one-way street.** So often, candidates approach interviews from the perspective that it's all about making a good impression on the interviewers, but that's only half the equation. An interview is actually about determining whether you are a good fit for the company AND whether the company is a good fit for you. If you have reservations during the interview process, it is possibly a sign that the organization isn't the right option.

2- **You have the right to walk away.** An interview is a chance to get to know the company and how they work. In this case, and in another anecdote later in the chapter, I realized that the company's culture simply wasn't a good fit for me. Instead of wasting everyone's time by seeing the interview process through to the bitter end, I took myself out of contention for the job at stake. I took the risk to walk away and hold out for something better suited to me, and I believe that I saved myself potential years of trying to fit into a workplace that didn't suit my needs.

There Is No Corporate Ladder

We are conditioned at school to believe that if we hit certain markers of success, including individual grades, GPA, and test scores, we will advance smoothly to the next level. Most of us carry that belief with us into the workforce, where, unfortunately, that just isn't the way the professional world works. You can "ace" the performance review but not get the promotion. You can do great in an interview and still not get hired. Many people dislike the idea of looking at career advancement in terms of learning to "play the game," but not doing so will put you at a disadvantage. We need to form alliances, self-promote, self-advocate, and play politics in some cases to get to where we want to be. Networking and getting feedback from multiple sources are action steps that help us crowdsource the relevant information to help us form the right allegiances and make the best moves to advance in our careers.

Women, in particular, are conditioned from a young age that playing the "good girl" and following all the rules will get us recognized for our accomplishments. There is a persistent idea in the analogy of a "corporate ladder" to the top, and that good employees will climb the rungs one by one, which puts women at a disadvantage. I think about career progression as being like a game of Chutes and Ladders. It was my favorite board game growing up. Candy Land was a very close second. The general premise was that if you landed on a square where there was a positive action, like cutting the lawn or rescuing a kitty, you got rewarded with a trip up the ladder, getting you closer to the finish line. If you landed on a square with a negative action, like eating a whole box of chocolates or breaking a window, you had to take the chute down further from the finish line.

Consider this variation when thinking about your career, except take the negativity out of the chute. You don't hit a chute by doing something wrong. In a blog post by Kelly Ford, he states, "Chutes and ladders can *both* connect you to future opportunities. **Chutes** represent continuity & transferring skills or knowledge from a previous position. They represent the things you've already done that can get you a new job. **Ladders** involve doing something different to broaden your skill set and give you more options in the future." Early in your career, you will likely have more opportunities for chutes—parallel job opportunities allowing you to deepen your skills and expand your perspective. A chute allows you to transition your current skill set to a similar role in a different department or company. A ladder allows you to take the skills you have and then build up a level.

My first three jobs were "analyst" jobs, working in the weeds of something. I started as a pricing analyst focused on costing, large pricing data sets, and spreadsheets. I took a chute to another company as a systems analyst, working with developers and structured datasets to create operations reports for leadership. And my last chute before I had a ladder opportunity was as a business analyst working between customers and developers to develop a new software product.

When I look back at the various roles I had, it wasn't all ladders and fancy job titles. Like most professionals, my job history is a mix of ups and downs, all leading me in the direction of my current role as founder of TGR Management Consulting. Setbacks are inevitable, but they can help you see in which direction you should be moving next.

Rejection

How Hard Is It To Find Work?

Unless you are extremely fortunate or happen to stumble upon the right job at the right time, you are going to face rejection in your job search. Research shows that the average person goes through 10-20 interviews before being hired. Read that number again because I had to read it twice myself. 10-20 interviews is the *average*. So, if you feel you've been striking out over and over, you're not alone.

We've talked about handling rejection throughout the book, so by now, you have some strategies for dealing with disappointment. However, dealing with rejection 10 to 20 times in a short period while looking for work, often when we're already feeling stressed and vulnerable, is harder than normal. So, let's talk about some interview strategies that can help make it more likely that you will be one of the exceptions and land a job quickly. To do that, you may need to change how you approach interviews.

My best piece of advice is only two words long: **Play offense**.

Resumes and cover letters can only get you so far. Algorithms look for keywords that may get you through to the interview stage, and then you have to do the rest. You should do some research on what those keywords are for each role, and you should resist the urge to make up your own words and titles. Potential employers only know what you tell them, so prepare in advance with additional anecdotes and examples of work that you've done that has made a positive impact in your current role. Being shy, humble, or embarrassed to talk yourself up will get you nowhere. Use professional language, deliver the information in a matter-of-fact tone, and own your contributions.

When I interview prospective team members, I want to feel confident that the person I'm hiring is motivated, skilled, and will be an asset to my team, not a liability. While there's always an on-the-job training component, I want people who seek out opportunities and are proactive in figuring out how things work and where they can make the most impact. It's not always possible to get all of that out of an interview, but I am definitely impressed when a candidate comes prepared and has some relevant, thoughtful questions for me that go beyond the basics.

The typical interviewer usually spends 75% of the time asking questions to get a better sense of how you will fit into their role, team, and company and usually leaves 25% of the time for you. It is your chance to steer the conversation in your favor, to get beyond the job description, and to discuss many of the topics already covered in this book. Many interviews focus on behaviors, asking about specific situations you've faced to gauge how you behave. You spend a lot of time with your co-workers, and the interviewer wants to know how your style fits with the team. Be prepared with three examples or stories highlighting the behaviors you want them to know that can be used to answer a question that starts with "Tell me about a time…" The best defense is a good offense!

Below are some of my favorite interview questions. If you aren't asking, you are missing an opportunity to clarify expectations.

- What are the major goals for your new hire this year and next year?

- What are the top goals of the company over the next 12 months?

- How does the role tie into those company goals?

- What constitutes a workday here? When do people typically start and stop working?

- How do you like to communicate with the folks on your team?

- Can you tell me a story that illustrates your management style?

- Do you do one-on-one meetings? How often do those take place?

- How do you handle performance and salary reviews here?

- I work hard during the week and take weekends off. What's your stance on reachability after-hours and/or after-hours meetings?

Don't assume the interviewer is good at leading an interview. If you find the conversation is stalling and there are awkward pauses, try asking one of the questions below to help build quick rapport.

- I'd love to hear your career story. How did you come to be here in this job?

- What are some of your team's biggest accomplishments over the past year or so?

- What do you like about working here?

I've also had more than one interview where I didn't get the chance to ask questions because the interviewer was late or took the whole time talking. It's OK to ask for more time, and if they are "too busy," it could be an indication of something more.

If you are trying to land that next-level role (a ladder position), be sure to ask questions that demonstrate your ability to think at that next level. For example:

- A lot of managers of this function struggle with XX - is that an issue here, too?

- From my research, issues/trends X, Y, and Z might be high on your priority list. Have you seen that here? I'd love to get your perspective.

If you aren't used to asking these types of detailed questions during interviews, it can feel awkward at first, but it's worth moving past that feeling. It might not go as smoothly as you'd like the first time, but it will get easier. I often interview people with resumes that, for the most part, are almost exactly the same in terms of the type of education and experience. It is especially true with entry-level jobs but can also hold true with upper level jobs whose specialized nature means that most people have a lot of crossover in skills and experience. The candidate who shows the most interest in the inner workings of the company and the position is the one who typically makes the biggest impression.

That impression can pay off even if you don't get the job you interview for. It's not unheard of for hiring managers to keep a person's resume or connect with them on a social platform to stay in touch if they did exceptionally well in the interview but lost out to another candidate for the job. They can be referred to another department or called back if something comes up at a later date. As I've said in the past, a No is sometimes really a Not Yet.

Resilience

When Is It Worth Holding Out For Something Better?

I have had my share of interviews, which means I've seen the good along with the bad. Let's be honest; no one needs to be prepared for a great interview. It's the weird, uncomfortable, or just plain BAD ones that we need to be prepared for. In the early 2000s, I was employed with a large healthcare company. When I moved across the country, I was looking to take a step up in my career with another healthcare company. I had gotten a bit bored with the role I was in and felt that along with the move, a larger career role would also be a good idea.

I was interviewing for a program management office position which would have been a step up from the role I had recently left, working directly with the executive leader, fairly high up in the organization. The role was narrowed down to me and another candidate, an internal one. I was brought back for interview after interview, seven times. SEVEN interviews! The hiring manager, an executive leader, just could not decide.

When they invited me back for an 8th interview, I said no. I took myself out of the running for the job.

What happened next is something I've never experienced at any other point in my career. The executive was quite surprised that I would decline the opportunity to come in for yet another interview. He was not prepared for me to turn the role down, and he lectured me on how inappropriate it was to do so. Telling me how I had wasted *his* time interviewing for a role that *I* wasn't serious about. He then stated that I probably wouldn't have been a good fit anyway since I was walking away when things got hard, implying that I wouldn't have been able to cut it in the role.

It was disappointing to walk away from what could have been an excellent career opportunity, but I trusted my intuition. If it was so difficult for this leader to make a choice between one internal and one external candidate for a job that required eight rounds of interviews, it spoke volumes about the internal decision-making processes and inefficiencies I was likely to encounter in the company. I had already laid all my cards on the table and didn't have anything more to add, so continuing to go in over and over *was* wasting everyone's time.

I talk about this particular interview in the resilience section because everything about the experience demanded resilience on my part. Moving from one state to another and leaving a good job in a well-known company before securing work elsewhere in a bad economy all required me to stay resilient and strong and to trust in the process. The interview process demanded resilience of a different kind.

Being called back to a second or even a third interview for a high-level position isn't at all unheard of, and for some roles, is to be expected. It's nerve-wracking for some, requires patience for all, and is part of the process. I've never heard of anyone being called back for eight interviews, particularly not once the pool had already been narrowed down to two candidates. Looking back, if I had been in a different set of circumstances, I wouldn't have gone back the seven times that I did! It was tough being put through that kind of scrutiny, and it was also a bit demoralizing each time I got called back. I knew I was good at what I did and would have been a good fit for the position, but I was also aware that internal candidates often have the advantage in these scenarios. Keeping my hopes up and a good attitude became more difficult with every round.

I ultimately decided that despite everything, it wasn't the role or the company for me. It meant starting the job search over from scratch again, but I knew that I was better off walking away. It takes a lot of courage to walk away from the potential of a high-profile or lucrative job, but it takes even more to have the resilience to believe that it's worth it to wait for the right opportunity.

Reset

You've sent out your resume, leveraged your professional network, been to more interviews than you can count, handled rejection, and stayed resilient.

And you still don't have a job.

It's time for a reset. If the usual tactics aren't working, it's time to switch things up. It's natural to look for work in the areas that are most closely related to our current profession. Moving up in a company, applying for work with a competitor, or networking via our professional contacts are all the most usual, logical approaches. That doesn't mean they're the only approaches. It can be scary to step out of your comfort zone and be open to completely new opportunities, but just because it's scary doesn't mean it's bad.

Consider non-traditional networking opportunities. Women in the last two decades are more educated and at higher levels than at any point in history. Whether we have chosen careers or work in the home, we have experiences, and we know people. So why aren't we networking with each other the way that men do?

Women are great connectors. We connect with other men and women on the sidelines, in the church group, or in the Girl Scout troop. We get to know people by volunteering to supervise field trips, community events, or donation drives. We expand our networks through walking clubs, book clubs, and group exercise classes. And we need to reframe these opportunities for what they are: networking.

We are great at networking to find a plumber...why not a job? The number of connections available to us that we overlook because they are casual, informal, or not based on work is putting women at a disadvantage. When we look at those connections from a more strategic standpoint, we may find that there are several opportunities ripe for exploring.

One of my favorite leadership books is called *The Female Advantage* by Sally Helgesen. The book was originally published in 1990, and I read it in the early 2000s. I don't remember what made me buy it, but I've read it multiple times, and over 30 years later, I still find it relevant. Helgesen maintains that women often build "webs" rather than hierarchies, relying on the authentic connections they make with others to help move forward. We build connections at the human level, whether in person, in print, or on social media. We've been doing it for years, one small interaction at a time. So, when was the last time you used the human connection that you built to help you professionally?

Chapter Summary

- Rather than thinking of career advancement as climbing the rungs of a corporate ladder in a linear fashion, approach it like a game of Chutes and Ladders where progression isn't always linear but can often advance in great leaps.

- Interviews are not only for the company to decide if they like the candidate. They are also for the candidate to get a better idea if the company and the role are a good fit. If not, the candidate can elect to remove themself from the selection process.

- Play offense in interviews. Be more than prepared; be prepared to make the interviewers see your past accomplishments and future potential. Have thoughtful, relevant questions prepared.

- Network in untraditional ways. Leverage your non-professional contacts. Reframe casual encounters and see the opportunities you may have overlooked because they presented themselves in unorthodox ways.

Chapter 7

Reacclimating After a Leave: The Tough Transition Back

Aside from the occasional sprained ankle and broken wrist because I took a pick-up game a little too seriously, I have been extremely fortunate in my life journey to be healthy. That good grace has extended to my family. Most of my time off work has been for common reasons: vacations and kids with runny noses. My only leaves of absence were maternity-related, and I was lucky to live in a state that offered additional consideration to both working parents.

Not unlike many career-driven women, I tried to be strategic in the timing of starting my family. I wanted to be settled in my career, marriage, and finances. I can hear my Grandma Millie chuckling as I write. She often said, "Oh, Tiffy Ann, if you want to hear God laugh, tell Him YOUR plan," when I would pontificate on some scheme I had hatched as a child. Yep, I had it all worked out.

About five years into our marriage, things were going well. We owned a home and had well-paying jobs … Check, check, check, down the list. Naturally, we felt it was time to start our family. We had extended family inquiring as to when it was going to happen! My husband's grandfather called on the regular to ask how long we were going to make him wait to meet a great-grandchild, telling us he wasn't going to live forever. No pressure.

Not unlike many women, I discovered it wasn't as easy to get pregnant as I had anticipated. I had imagined things going differently, according to *my* plan. It was a solid nine months of disappointment before success, which felt like a failure and an eternity. I know that many couples endure years of disappointment and that nine months is minor, but it was difficult for me emotionally.

During that time, we kept our pregnancy difficulties to ourselves. We didn't want any additional input into what was turning into an increasingly stressful situation. The question, "When will you have a baby?" was not helpful. Some women openly share their pregnancy journey with others, but that isn't my style. Other women are forced to be open about it due to IVF treatments, insurance issues, or missed days at work. The desire for privacy and the ability to have it is not always granted.

During that period, I was promoted and given more responsibilities at work. As a result, I was especially intentional about not sharing any personal news in the office. I was a fully remote employee for a fabulous software company in Ohio. When I became pregnant, I was terrified to tell my colleagues despite working for an inviting, supportive company. I was occasionally required to travel to the corporate office, and every time, there was always welcome and warmth. Business travel can be a lonely experience. At this company, I never dined alone. My coworkers would meet me for breakfast, plan a happy hour, or organize a dinner. I had one coworker who, if her home situation would allow for nothing else—would always find our way to Graeter's for ice cream. Who says "no" to ice cream?

I worked for a female manager, Stephanie, for a few years. We had a great relationship, and I truly loved working for her. Stephanie was everything I wanted to be as I grew in my career: smart, accomplished, respected, kind in the workplace, and equally had it together outside as wife, mother, and community member. She made it all look easy. Despite all of that office sunshine and rainbows, those coworkers were the last to know about my pregnancy. Why? Because I was afraid of what it might mean for the change in my career trajectory. I've heard the same tales and read the same opinion pieces you have. Real or perceived, even in my situation, I was petrified of the reaction to my pregnancy.

Looking back now, I'm not sure *my grand plan* had a plan for telling my coworkers I was pregnant. I never thought about how I would communicate it. My boss and I talked daily and shared what we did each weekend and other mundane things. Was I supposed to drop my life and career-changing nugget of news between the weather and weekend highlights on a Monday? Or should I wait until a really hard day and position it as the day's good news?

My husband and I shared our good news first with family and close friends, but somehow, saying those words out loud to my coworkers was different. It took me a while to find the words—five months, to be exact. A required visit to the corporate office finally forced my announcement.

That was it. I would either show up "showing," or I could give a little warning that I would show up "showing." Either way, the news was going to be out there soon. I decided I needed to call Stephanie directly. I don't remember anything about the conversation (after all my worry, not a single word) other than she was ecstatic. The news spread faster than I was ready for, and there was welcome and warmth each time.

Despite the overwhelmingly positive reaction I received from my manager and coworkers, the point I want to make here is how this particular scenario is specific to women. The changes in my body were not possible to hide forever. Similarly, if a woman changes her name after marriage or divorce, she is essentially forced into disclosing personal information she may not be comfortable sharing. I had a supportive work environment, but not everyone can say the same.

Some weeks later, when I was in the office, we sat down to talk through what my maternity leave would look like. My manager had many questions for me that I had no answer to.

How many weeks was I going to take off? Did I want to work right up to the last second? She had done so when she was pregnant. Her water broke in the office, and we had a good laugh at how that played out. Even though I was a remote employee, she didn't advise that for me. We roughly settled on taking my leave the week before my due date, and as things got closer, we made adjustments. She wanted me to have closure at the office and not bring any unfinished work stress into the labor and delivery.

When we were a week away, most of my responsibilities were wrapped up or transitioned to someone else. It was weird; there were a few days when I went to work and had nothing to do. Stephanie insisted that I remove email from my phone and not log in to "check" on anything when I was out. She put my husband's cell phone number on a sticky note on her monitor (where all her important reminders went) so she could bug him for updates.

Throughout my twelve weeks of leave, Stephanie called every ten days or so to ask for pictures and give me the office update. She'd ask how I was doing, and when I gave her the rosy answer, she'd tell me a less-than-flattering new mom story from her early days. When I finally confessed that breastfeeding was hard and I was awful at it, she reassured me that I'd figure it out and that I couldn't be as bad at that as I was at bowling (truth and a story for another time). She would also remind me that she was saving a fantastic bag of chaos for me to open when I returned but wouldn't get into any details, so I *would* actually return!

I took 12 weeks of maternity leave. It was consistent with company policy, and financially, it was all we could afford. Additional time would have been uncompensated. Fortunately, after 12 weeks, I was physically, mentally, and emotionally ready to return to work. It is personal to every woman, but the timing was right for me. My husband and I had gotten into a routine with the baby. We had found childcare, and I was succeeding in some combination of breastfeeding and pumping. I was finding time to work out and finally sleeping more than two hours at a time. It was hard, but it wasn't impossible. We were figuring it out.

The unanticipated benefit for me when I returned to work was that I was a fully remote employee. There were no video calls, no squeezing into work clothes, no finding hiding places to pump, no embarrassing leaks, no exhausting commute... I could go on. My return to work challenges were fractional by comparison to other parents. And yet, it was still a struggle to "schedule" pumping (in the privacy of my own home) during the work day, adjust to an Eastern time zone work schedule while living the family life in Pacific time, and make it through the day without a nap. My initial weeks back in the office were boring. I had transitioned all my prior work away, and Stephanie was still holding the strings to the bag of chaos she had promised. She was slowly assigning tasks to me, asking me lots of questions, and checking in often, ensuring things were going well (at work and home).

In hindsight, I fully appreciate her genius and generosity in the approach. She had been investing in my return before I even went on leave. She was building my confidence in this new life skill, alleviating my career fears by keeping me connected to my professional self, and slowly bringing me back, ensuring I had the support system at home to pull the weight at work. The process took a few months, and she promoted me to a manager role as soon as I was ready. I was leading that team of coworkers, which was the hardest promotion I've had (and a story for another chapter).

That was the help I needed.

What I didn't understand, and couldn't until I was nearly through it, was the number of potential failure points in my return to work. Stephanie clearly understood them, being a few years removed from it herself. At the time, I didn't think of all the things that could go wrong. I could have had medical complications, or worse, the baby could have had medical complications. Many women suffer from postpartum depression, and the lack of consistent childcare options could have limited my ability to return to work. All things that would have severely limited my ability to return not only to employment but to my pre-pregnancy, over-achieving, work-loving self. Once I returned to work,

Stephanie understood that my adjustment was more of a marathon than a sprint. I needed to build back up to that first full day, week, and month. The rise early, put on the Mom cape, then tuck it under the work outfit to become the employee/manager/ team member, then bring it out again at the late evening hours pace was a lot. I would still be all those other things—but the Mom cape was never coming off.

Leaves of absence come in several forms, including but not limited to pregnancy, illness, disability, or family care. Some are short-term, while others are long-term; some are planned, while many are unplanned or emergency leaves. The type and duration of leave create unique challenges, opportunities, and hurdles for leaving and re-entering the workforce after a career break. It can be difficult for both the employee and employer, so it's important to consider certain things when taking a leave and when returning from one. Regardless of how dedicated you are to your career, it is only one part of the larger puzzle, which is your life. Sometimes, personal circumstances require your undivided attention for a certain period.

Short-Term Leaves

Some short-term leaves are planned, such as parental leaves. Leave allowance for women varies by state, but maternity leave in the U.S. is generally less than six months. In many states, it's six weeks! Pregnancy, in general, signals significant changes are coming for an employee, which can itself provoke concerns about how their employer will view them. A full 21% of mothers report having been afraid to tell their employers about their pregnancy for fear of discrimination or retaliation.

Long-Term Leaves

Long-term leaves, for the purposes of this chapter, are a year or longer. They may be taken as sabbaticals to pursue continuing education, for personal illness or disability, for taking care of a family member, or for other valid reasons. Long-term leaves can be huge adjustments for both employee and employer as the longer someone is away from the work environment, the more complex the readjustment period can be upon their return.

Women take more "career breaks" than men and for much different reasons. Of the top 7 reasons women take leave, full-time parenting is number 1, and caregiving is number 3. For men, full-time parenting is number 7, and caregiving doesn't even make the list.

In this chapter, I'll help show you how to leverage this transition as a springboard for personal and professional growth. Since the impact of short-term leaves is much different than long-term ones, I'll split the content in this chapter between leaves of less than a year, whether planned or unplanned, and leaves of one year or more. It doesn't matter how long you're gone from work; it's imperative to realize that **you will return a changed person**.

When I first went back to the office after pregnancy leave, there were both physical and mental switches that I had to learn to turn on and off between work and home. For example, I used to sway when standing up because that's what I had done while holding my baby for months. It had become an automatic habit when standing. **There's a mental load that you carry as a caregiver.** I struggled to focus on solving the work problem in front of me because my brain was busy trying to solve a logistical problem at home. Problems like, How could I rearrange my afternoon so I could get to the grocery store for diapers and formula on my way home from work but before picking up my son from daycare? It's a constant ping-ponging of thoughts solutioning for work and home, and it's exhausting. The mental load is hard for others to understand if they don't have the same caregiver situation or don't have the same level of responsibility as a caregiver as you do.

That said, there are a lot of crossover skills developed by juggling things like caregiving and work that can be put to advantage in the workplace. I have a speech I've given in the past about getting the company to think about strategy, and it looks like getting my family to give me dinner ideas! Here's a common scenario at my house. Around 8:00 am, I'll ask everyone what they want for dinner and receive a typical response of, "It's way too early to be thinking about dinner." At noon, the question takes on more urgency. After all, I may still need to buy ingredients. Yet the response becomes, "I just finished lunch. I can't think about dinner yet!" At 3:00 pm, suddenly, everyone wants to know, "Hey, Mom, what's for dinner?" Once we finally decide, there's a mad scramble to get to the store, cook the meal, and coordinate who's eating and when because we have many other priorities.

Does this sound familiar?

The same scenario happens in companies. During the first quarter, everyone's thinking about planning. By the second quarter, some good ideas are dictated by the market. Finally, someone asks, "Hey, what are our yearly sales goals?" It is followed by a mad scramble to develop a plan, plus implementation… but it's already quarter three. Comparing meal planning and strategic planning is simplifying things a little, but the underlying skills remain the same. Running a household and family is no joke, and many logistics tend to fall on women. Why not leverage those skills in the workplace to your advantage?

Risk

Taking a leave can feel risky. Change is always hard, and change on the scale of leaving a job, even temporarily, can invoke feelings of anxiety or fear. **Concerns around employment and employability are very valid and real.**

Individuals may worry about how potential employers will view their time away from the workforce or whether it will impact their employability. They may worry about whether they will be able to return and work at the same level they could before their leave. There may be a fear of being stigmatized or stereotyped based on the reason for the career break, such as maternity leave or caregiving responsibilities. Returnees may fear that the break will hinder their career trajectory, leading to concerns about advancement opportunities. Employees may also fear strained relationships with colleagues or supervisors due to the perceived burden of maternity (or other) leave on team dynamics and workload distribution.

If you are also worried about taking a leave, know you're not alone. Research shows that 31% of U.S. workers fear repercussions, such as getting fired or passed over for a promotion if they do. Additionally, 29% believe a negative perception is associated with taking leave in general. The fear could lead to people putting off taking a leave, even in situations such as illness, which could have negative consequences for their health or their personal life.

I believe the percentages could be much higher than reported. When someone goes out on leave, a company rarely replaces that employee with a temporary worker. There are many logical and financially justifiable reasons for not hiring a contractor to assume the responsibilities of a person on leave. However, it is equally rare to have coworkers with extra capacity to manage your work while you are out.

When I've been the manager responsible for assigning work to other team members to cover an employee's extended absence, I've found the rub to be how frequently the same person on the team is asked to assume that additional responsibility. And women who don't have kids will tell you that it disproportionately falls on them to pick up the slack. Regardless of your role in the leave of absence, be thoughtful when planning the "who" is getting asked to assume more responsibility and how many times it has happened in the past. Asking someone to stretch their skills may maintain better harmony in the team than asking the same person to stretch their personal time. Again.

Returning to Work After a Short Career Break

Many of the concerns that people have when returning after taking long career breaks are less relevant following short ones. It's highly unlikely that technology or skills have evolved to the point of feeling left behind, and professional networks should still mostly be intact. The business has matured and you still need to get caught up on the changes in processes, policies, and technology. The crux of the risk in returning following short-term leaves tends to be more on a personal level: Will I be able to do my job as well as I could before? Can I handle performing at the same pace as before with my new responsibilities? Learning to balance priorities in a new way can take some time to get right. Juggling work responsibilities with potential caregiving duties or other personal commitments can create stress and overwhelm.

The fear of making mistakes is not specific to work but also to what you leave behind at home. If you are returning from maternity leave, those first few months leaving your baby with someone else can be anxiety-producing. Physical and mental exhaustion can make it complicated to perform personal and professional duties to the same standard. Fear of being judged is also very real. Are your coworkers helping you with that project because they understand your situation and want to be supportive, or do they think you're no longer capable?

It's also unrealistic to think that your brain will be fully in the game immediately. Suppose you took a short leave to care for an ill family member, or due to a short but significant illness, or any other life-altering event. In that case, you may be returning to work with some trauma, lingering physical symptoms, or increased responsibilities at home that can make jumping right back into the office environment difficult.

Returning to Work Following a Long Career Break

Longer breaks come with all of the above concerns, as well as a few more! I consider a long-term leave to be anything over one year, which is enough time for fairly significant changes to happen in a workplace, industry, or the economy. Companies restructure, key people come and go, and processes can evolve to look little like they did before you left.

One of the biggest concerns when returning to work after a long period away is the skill gap. Technology and industry standards may have evolved during the break, leading to a perceived gap in skills or knowledge. If there is concern you may no longer be up-to-date on key skills needed to perform your role, discuss it with your manager before returning to work to sort out a plan to get you up to speed. There's no one-size-fits-all response. It's in both your and your employer's best interests to agree on a plan beforehand and to plan a turnover time period as well. This is the number of days/weeks/months you might need to adjust to the workplace and learn any new tools or skills to be successful. I know that managers and HR want to keep good people. It makes more sense to support good employees than to hire new ones, so don't hesitate to ask for what you need.

Reintegration into a job and wider industry after more than a year away requires rebuilding professional networks and re-establishing oneself within the workplace culture, which can be daunting. Your former influence may no longer exist, and you may no longer be the go-to person for certain things. People you worked with or knew in the industry in the past may have moved up or moved on, making you feel a bit left behind. It's normal and will usually dissipate over time.

Setting up time during your away period to stay in contact with your network and up-to-date on the industry can help reduce anxiety on both being gone and returning in the know. Even if you do this only a few hours in the month before you return, it signals to the people involved that you are receptive to the shift back.

Rejection

Not all leaves end well. Sometimes, the employee can't return to work in the same capacity and struggles to resume their duties or chooses another path that better suits their changed needs. Other times, the employer is less than accommodating upon return, or even annoyed that the employee took the leave in the first place, and refuses to offer any support beyond the bare minimum. Discrimination does happen, and it can be difficult to work through. Sometimes, it is subtle enough to have you questioning if it's real. If you are feeling unsupported or treated unfairly, there are steps you can take.

Workplace Discrimination and Career Progression

Employees returning from leave often worry about being treated differently in the workplace. These fears are often unfounded, but unfortunately, cases of workplace discrimination and delayed career progression exist.

There is a risk of being confronted by stereotypes about commitment or capability after returning from leave.

Questions of commitment may follow a leave in which you were caring for a newborn baby or an ill or disabled family member, particularly since the caregiving responsibility is often ongoing even upon return to work. Women often take on more of the burden of childcare and family care, resulting in sometimes having their commitment to their job questioned upon return from a leave. Questions of the capability to perform their previous role are more likely to follow a leave that was taken for personal health or disability reasons. Employers and colleagues may question if a returnee is completely healed from an illness or whether they can perform their job if they have recently acquired a disability. These concerns can be detrimental and lead to discriminatory and illegal behavior.

Although the expectation is that following a leave, you will return to the same position you left, it is not always the case. Sometimes, a role is eliminated or given to two other employees to share. Other times, the person returns to the same role, but it has changed so significantly that it is not recognizable. It's not unheard of for employees to be assigned a different role at the same pay grade, but that is nothing like what they did before the leave. It can lead to frustration, poor performance, and conflict in the workplace. Sometimes, the returning employee is overlooked for pay raises, promotions, or other career advancements for a certain period. In rare cases, the returning employee is laid off or let go before the return to work date or shortly after that.

Responding to Unfair Treatment

If you do end up on the receiving end of unfair or illegal treatment, there are steps you can take to protect yourself. They are a good place to start if you have a good relationship with your manager and have general concerns. If that is not the case, or your manager is part of the problem, consider another path, either with HR or a level above your manager if you already have that relationship established.

1- **Know Your Rights:** Familiarize yourself with employment laws and policies regarding maternity or other leaves and discrimination. You may have to become familiar with both federal and state laws. Don't overlook official company policies around leaves as well. Many HR departments have specific training in this area and can also answer any questions you may have.

2- **Document Everything:** Keep records of discriminatory behavior or unfair treatment for potential future recourse. It's important to keep solid written records that include dates, times, individuals involved, circumstances, and a description of what has occurred. Trying to recall details mentally at a later date is not always reliable. Having a chronological record (that is not on a company-controlled work computer, phone, or cloud storage) can help establish the frequency and severity of incidents if there is a pattern of behavior or discrimination.

3- **Seek Support:** Most companies have different avenues for employees to report workplace discrimination concerns. Reach out to HR, EAPs (employee assistance programs), unions, or legal counsel for guidance and support in addressing instances of discrimination. Professional groups or other advocacy groups can provide unbiased information and resources.

4- **Advocate for Change:** When you are in a position to do so, mentally and professionally. However, we can all behave more inclusively toward others in the workplace returning from leave and trying to settle back in. Work toward promoting a more inclusive and supportive workplace culture that values diversity and accommodates employee life transitions.

Resilience

Best Practices to Consider

Returning to work following any type of leave can feel like many things are out of your control. You can counter this feeling by planning your return as carefully as possible. I consider the following suggestions part of the resilience needed to organize your return and readapt to the work environment. We often expect to smoothly restart our careers following a prolonged absence, but that is rarely how it goes. **It's normal to feel like an outsider for a while, readjusting to the hours, the pace, and the expectations of**

your old job while the life circumstances surrounding it are no longer the same. Give yourself some grace and be patient with yourself while you readapt.

Be prepared that your colleagues, particularly those without the experience of raising kids, may believe that you *will* be the same person when you return. If Sally has been covering my work for the last three months, she may expect that I will be ready to take it all back by day three of my return, either because that's what she's been told by leadership or that's what she's been telling herself the whole time.

1- **Discuss your return with your manager ahead of time.** What scenario would work best for everyone? A gradual return, or jumping back in full-time right away? Perhaps a few days of reintroduction to the role would be helpful. **Also, consider announcing your return to your colleagues in advance via email.** Having a solid grasp of the expectations for your return before you walk back into the workplace can help calm nerves and encourage a smooth transition. This includes expectations both for you and for others about you!

2- **Don't assume that everything will be the same.** Return to work with fresh eyes and a willingness to learn what's changed. There may be processes and procedures you were familiar with that are now outdated. People may have shifted roles or taken on different responsibilities, or a change in leadership could mean that the role you left is much different than the one you return to, even if the title stays the same. Trying to return to the way things were before you left is a recipe for disaster.

3- **Take Time to Adjust.** Reassess how you used to do things in accordance with how they are done now. It's easy to get sucked into thinking that you need to get up to speed on everything immediately, but that's not necessarily the case. Identify, preferably in coordination with your team leader, the top three priorities and start there.

Reset

The most important part of resetting your career following a leave is understanding that you are not going back to work the same person you were when you left, and you are not returning to the same work environment either. It may look the same at first glance, but subtle shifts always take place over time that will take some getting used to. Give yourself some grace to find your groove again. Connect with management or HR ahead of time, consider making a few short scheduled visits before your official return date to get the feel of things, and be patient with yourself when things go wrong. It's a learning curve, not unlike starting the job from scratch all over again.

That said, changing life situations can often mean a change in goals. You may return to work after a leave, relieved to be back and ready to pick up exactly where you left off, or you might not. If your priorities have changed, be honest with yourself and update your career goals. The best time to reassess your career goals is while you are on leave, assuming you have the time to dedicate to it. It can save a lot of hardship and frustration if you decide before returning to your old job that you would really rather be doing something else or working part-time, for example.

Sometimes, we don't realize that our old jobs are no longer right for us until we return and realize that we don't feel the same anymore or that our new personal circumstances are no longer conducive to our role at work. Assess your new wants and needs, and consider whether or not they are feasible in the company you work for. Consider a career counselor or speak to HR about various options. **Being proactive is key**. It's better for you to take the initiative and generate options than to be laid off or fired because you are not meeting expectations.

It's normal to experience frustrations and setbacks in the return phase. Build a support network and seek support from family, friends, and colleagues to navigate the challenges of returning to work after a leave.

Chapter Summary

- It is normal to feel worried, conflicted, or anxious before taking a leave of absence from your job.

- If you are being treated unfairly, document everything, seek support, and advocate for change where possible.

- Do not expect everything to return to how it was before you left. Expect an adjustment period and give yourself time to get back into the swing of things.

- Consider reassessing your personal and professional goals before returning from leave and within a few months of being back on the job to decide if some need to be reset.

Chapter 8

Reframing the Narrative: Managing Motherhood and Career

I was in the 11th week of my third pregnancy, packing for another business trip, when it happened. Nearly five years had passed since my second child had been born, and he was off to school in the fall. Having kids in school is a huge milestone and a win for working parents. My husband and I were moving along in life, figuring it would be if it were meant to be. So when I found out we'd be going from a man-to-man defense with two kids to a zone defense with three kids, almost five years after the last one, I wasn't quite sure how I felt. We hadn't told anyone yet and planned to visit family a few weeks later. We were excited to be able to tell people in person this time!

Having recently survived a company reorganization, I was working on building a relationship with a new manager. Stephanie had survived, too, but had a new team. My team (what was left of it) and I were eager to get focused on the new responsibilities. We had planned a team-building event in the corporate office. My team was located in all corners of the U.S., and our division leader was in Michigan, so Ohio was the logical choice.

Two days before the big team-building event, I had a medical emergency. I had lost the baby. To say it was crushing doesn't begin to cover it.

It was a Thursday, and I needed to tell people urgently. And not only people I was close with; I needed to tell the office that not only was I not getting on that plane on Sunday, but I needed time off immediately. After collecting myself, I called the one person I trusted the most professionally, Stephanie. My new manager was a nice man, but I didn't know him well and had no idea how I would tell him this information. I hadn't even planned to tell him I was pregnant until months later. I was relieved when Stephanie answered the phone. I tearfully shared what was happening and leaned on her to decide what to do next.

To be perfectly honest, I didn't want to tell anyone. It was my pain, and I didn't want to share it. I was emotional, and I wanted no one's sympathy. Except I needed to suddenly let my colleagues in on something so personal and painful. Stephanie was masterful at offering empathy and building confidence at the same time. I knew the phone call I had to make next.

I kept it short, matter-of-fact, and distant. I was trying to keep my emotions in check. My new boss was understanding but had no words. Nor was I expecting him to; it wasn't in the manager manual. He felt strongly that we needed to cancel the whole team-building event. I didn't want him to share the reason with the entire team. I wanted to choose to tell people in my own time. He agreed it was my news to share and assured me he wouldn't disclose my personal situation. So, I signed out for the day and tucked myself in bed with our dog.

Within a few hours, my phone buzzed with concerned coworker text messages. While my manager hadn't shared details of my miscarriage, he *had* sent an urgent email out to everyone on the team indicating that I had a "personal situation." He shared that I could no longer attend the team-building event and indicated that it would be rescheduled at a later date. Having recently gone through a reorganization in the company and my lack of online presence when that email came out, my team members panicked. Even Stephanie had dropped me a note saying the news wasn't landing well. My manager called me later to say that my colleagues weren't sure if I was sick, if I'd resigned, or if I'd been fired.

Even though he had reassured them that I was still with the company, he believed my team wanted to hear from me directly. He apologized for how things were playing out. On my end, I felt trapped by the entire situation. I had a right to my privacy according to every law and human resources, yet I felt that the reality was that I didn't in this particular situation. The illusion of control had disappeared. In the end, I put together a few sentences thanking everyone for their concerns, apologizing for disappointing them, and telling them I needed a few more days to "recover" and would be back to work soon.

This was NOT the help I needed.

Truthfully, I had no idea how long it would realistically take me to recover. The medical recovery was simple, and a few days later, I truly was back at work. The hormonal adjustments, however, took months, not days.

And then there was the grief. There's no real time limit on grief.

Returning to work as soon as I was *physically* cleared to do so did not give me the time I needed to recover mentally before picking up where I left off at work. There was no "ramping up" to full-time work or easing back into my duties, which made the transition more difficult than it needed to be.

After the birth of my other children, the medical and hormonal recovery happened while I was on leave and away from the workplace. It happened in private. This time, the emotional and hormonal recovery took place publicly while I was at work. It would ebb and flow at all times of the day, sometimes triggered and sometimes not. I couldn't control it and didn't want to explain it. I simply had to move through it.

From a management perspective, I believe we need to treat the return to work as an urgent or emergency situation

similar to a maternity leave. The employee needs time to transition back to the workplace full-time, understanding that just because the emergency has been taken care of doesn't mean that everything has gone back to normal. For example, an elderly parent who has a slip and fall incident may take a worker out of the office urgently for a short period of time to handle the emergency, but that doesn't mean that everything goes back to normal as soon as the employee returns to work. There may be months of management behind the scenes for that person to ensure the care of that elderly parent so that they can return to the workplace full-time.

I share my story because I believe that mothers in the workplace occupy a space distinct from their male colleagues or even their female colleagues who are not mothers or primary caregivers of children. I talked about leaves in general in Chapter 7, but I wanted to go more in-depth on motherhood in the workplace in a separate chapter.

The experiences of being a mother and a professional are chapter-worthy because motherhood permeates every area of life for as long as you live, unlike many other life changes. I know that not every woman wants to be a mother and that not everyone reading this chapter will agree with my views on juggling motherhood and a career. Still, I hope to provide useful insights and information based on my experiences. Not all of my experiences will still be the norm, as changes to workplace culture and legislation evolve continuously, and workplace regulations differ from state to state. Still, there are some universal challenges that all mothers face, and those are worth exploring.

Let's talk about the pressure mothers put on themselves to have it all done. I remember my first business trip after having my first child. Suddenly, business travel wasn't only about making sure I was packed and prepared. I felt I needed to prepare *everything* to hold the family over while I was away. I had never worried about what my husband would eat while I was traveling before, but suddenly, it felt important! I had taken the extra time (adding self-induced stress and pressure) in the days before leaving to make sure the fridge was stocked with food, there were diapers, the baby's clothes were washed, and the baby's outfits were laid out, all to make it easier on my husband. Why? Because I felt guilty that I was heading out of town.

What happened while I was gone? Nothing special. When I returned from the trip, my husband hadn't eaten any of the food I had left behind; some had spoiled and had to be thrown out. He also had yet to use the outfits I had laid out for the baby. I remember complaining about it to a friend (who didn't have kids), and her response was enlightening. She asked, Why did you feel the need to do all that? Does your husband not know where the grocery store is? Does it matter what outfit your infant shows up wearing in the daycare? It was a wake-up call. She was right. I had clearly focused on the wrong things out of guilt, worry, and the belief that I had to do it all.

This is where women often feel stressed. It's the constant "mom guilt" that ends up putting unnecessary pressure on ourselves to fit some unattainable perfect ideal. Men don't typically do this. When my husband has gone out of town, he has never once worried about my ability to feed myself or dress our children while he is gone!

Motherhood changes you as a woman, as a spouse/partner, as a friend, and certainly as an employee. Our bodies change. Our priorities shift. And our time is no longer our own to do with as we please. Some of these changes are positive and exciting, but others can come as a surprise and be frustrating or hard to deal with. On top of it all, women learn fairly quickly that motherhood changes how society at large perceives you as a human being. You are no longer the same person you were before you had children, and the whole world has opinions on what your role as a mother should look like. It often extends to the workplace and the views employers and colleagues may have about what it means to be a mother and a professional. And to be honest, they are contradictory!

Risk

The risk is that everything will change.

The truth is that it will.

But that doesn't mean it will all change for the worse. Being a mother is an amazing privilege, and while it can be challenging to juggle motherhood and work, it is possible to do both. As much as I have enjoyed all the seasons of my kids' development, I also get tremendous fulfillment from my work. Being a parent and having a career are not mutually exclusive, but I would be lying if I said that life just went on as usual post-children. Of course, it didn't. My whole world had changed. Just as I had to make significant adjustments in my private life to adapt to motherhood, I also had to adjust professionally. **One of the biggest adjustments was understanding that not everything can be the top priority at once, and some things that used to be important were now landing lower on the list.**

Nora Roberts was once asked how to balance writing and kids. She said that the key to juggling is to know that some of the balls you have in the air are made of plastic and some are made of glass..." She continued, "And if you drop a plastic ball, it bounces, no harm done. If you drop a glass ball, it shatters, so you have to know which balls are glass and which are plastic and prioritize catching the glass ones."

Societal Norms and Expectations

I recall quite clearly one of the first times that the societal expectations of mothers struck me, and the experience has stayed with me all these years. I consider myself lucky that I didn't feel the pressure of balancing work and family until my son went to kindergarten. I remember sitting in the *welcome to kinder* meeting at the school. There an implicit expectation that parents were expected to volunteer in the classroom regularly and contribute financially with supplies. On top of that, there were field trips for the children in which parents were expected to drive. Six of them! My five-year-old son was going on six field trips, and I was expected to drive him to and from them. Not only was I surprised that my young learner would be taken off campus many times in a single school year, but I was fired up over the expectation that my husband and I were simply supposed to figure out how to make it work.

The reality of the expectations of me as a mother hit home when I listened to another mother with an older child give advice specifically to the other mothers in the room. She advocated for working moms to talk to their employers about getting special time off or making other work adjustments so that they could volunteer in the classroom regularly. To be clear, she wasn't speaking to all the working parents, only to the other moms. The working moms. It tweaked me on so many levels!

As the year went on, I became more and more bitter about the expectations of the mothers in that class. Frankly, I couldn't keep up with the "momsmanship." I had working mom guilt already, and the one-upping that was taking place in the school brought it in buckets. Over time, I eventually found a way to contribute to my child's class and feel good about it, but it wasn't by taking more time off work to spend in the classroom or in ways that may have been externally obvious to my son or the other moms at the time. My children have now grown to understand and appreciate how I have contributed AND still gave them space in their classrooms and schools to develop some independence. That's not to say that it wasn't hard to push past the external expectations of my hands-on involvement during work hours and the feeling of being judged for choosing to make my career a priority.

It's important to have a realistic sense of what you want your journey to look like and then find the people in your life who will support you and help make that happen. I say "realistic" because, despite your best-laid plans, your journey doesn't always take you in the direction you expected. Or maybe you get there eventually, but the direct path you had charted turned out to be a winding road that took the scenic route. I am very fortunate to have a support network that meets me where I am. When I had two kids under the age of five, a friend with a son the same age would meet up with us at the park with a cooler of snacks. The kids would run off their excess energy, and we would talk it out. Don't overlook the other moms at your company. They have had or do have the same challenges and may have a solution for you!

Flexibility is key, particularly when it comes to navigating the unpredictable world of motherhood. When you encounter a roadblock or an unanticipated change in circumstances, work through the four Rs that I've built into every chapter: Risk, Rejection, Resilience, and Reset. Holding onto a vision of the future that no longer serves you or refusing to be flexible in how you meet your goal can work against you. Reassessing your current reality against the one you had planned for allows you to make the necessary adjustments to keep moving toward your goals.

Managing Work and Home

This is where many women struggle the most. Managing your expectations of what is possible with babies or children (even teens) in the house is key. The 5-9 before and after your 9-5 at work does not exist in the same way for working parents. The following may be a bit controversial, but in my decades of experience as a spouse, parent, employee, and businesswoman, I've come to see the following as generally true. I've also learned to be strategic in responding to each scenario.

- Those without the responsibility of raising children will out-work you, out-network you, out-play you, out-vacation you, and out-rest you.

- Going to evening career-advancing events more than once a week will create chaos at home.

- Your evenings and weekends will rarely be for "catching up on work." Instead, you will attend school events, cajole little people into taking baths, brushing their teeth, going to bed, and optimizing the family logistics of the week ahead.

- Those without job responsibilities will out-parent you. They will be at EVERY child event and will have been thoughtful enough to bake a healthy treat, considering all the food allergies in the class.

- You will have difficult/exhausting days at work and then have difficult/exhausting nights at home on the second shift.

- You will absolutely have a child get sick at the precise moment of the BIG meeting/deadline/presentation. It will likely require you to leave the office to pick them up or take them to a doctor's appointment.

And all of this will affect women more than it affects men. Times are changing, but the research still shows that women perform that "second shift" of home responsibilities more than men, which takes a toll. In 2022, 29% of marriages in the United States were considered "egalitarian," where the man and the woman each contribute between 40% and 60% of the household income. However, even in "egalitarian" marriages, women spent two hours more per week on caregiving and more than double their partners on housework.

The notion that women can do it all and have it all without sacrificing anything is not just wrong; it sets women up for burnout. It also sets them up to fall behind at work. Finding a balance that works for you is crucial. You will need to prioritize some areas over others. In Chapter 2, Crafting Your Compensation Story: Leveraging Your Value Beyond Salary, I talked about which feelings of guilt are most important for you to resolve (or quiet) and then communicate that to your manager and family. We'll discuss this in more detail in the Reset section below.

Perceptions of Motherhood in the Workplace

Many women worry there remains a risk of being perceived as less available, less committed, and less competent after becoming a mother. More and more companies are implementing family-friendly policies, but there are still many industries where motherhood is generally seen as incompatible with the job. I am also aware that my experience of being able to take months and not just weeks following the birth of my children is a luxury not every woman enjoys. One in four women in the United States return to work two weeks after giving birth, and only 13% of women in the private sector receive any paid leave at all. Many women return to work before their bodies have healed from childbirth.

Providing guidance in this particular area is a double-edged sword. There is no excuse for discrimination or unfair treatment by bosses or coworkers. Sometimes, the bias is more subtle. Bosses and coworkers might question your dedication to the job or wonder if you can still put in the same number of hours you used to. Taking time off when your child is sick or declining after-hours work events might raise some eyebrows if you were previously someone who participated in these types of activities. Continuing to present a professional image and work ethic can go a long way to reminding your colleagues of who you are as an employee.

Mothers are often given "grace" in many situations when it comes to kids, but I've also observed that many women don't recognize when they've reached the outer limit of that grace amongst their peers. Childless colleagues can often feel that they are not given the same leeway as parents are to take time off, leave early, or otherwise receive exemptions to certain expectations. For example, not arranging childcare when you return to work and thinking you can work from home and watch your baby simultaneously. Or consistently rescheduling meetings because babies don't keep meeting schedules.

It is also true with toddlers in daycare or children in school. They get sick often. As a parent, you must plan for when your child can't attend daycare or school because they are sick. Your employer might grant you the time off without a hassle for the first few ear infections, but eventually, that grace will wear thin. Most managers understand the challenges of parenthood to a certain extent. Still, eventually, the expectation is that you will handle your personal life outside the office, with the exception of emergencies.

In my experience, losing that "grace" has the most impact on your work relationships and creates doubt in your career progression. It could be why, for example, you aren't seeing glowing feedback from your peers in your performance reviews or that you aren't being selected for those key projects—and no one is willing to tell you the truth because they fear how it makes them look.

We, as women, can complain about how it shouldn't all fall on us. We're right, it shouldn't. But it often does. We can talk about how it should be cheaper to find help like childcare. It should. But it's not. I strongly support mothers in the workplace, and I have been thrilled to watch the evolution of younger couples sharing the load more equitably, but women still bear the brunt. While I encourage everyone to continue advocating for more support and family-friendly work policies and legislation, my goal in this book is to help you manage it all based on the realities of today. If you are in a situation where much of the responsibility falls to you, you need to own it and figure it out so that it doesn't negatively affect your career.

I know that it is a hard truth and uncomfortable to read, and I hope the day comes when it is no longer applicable. Companies are changing and adapting to new ways of doing business, including more family-friendly policies. Still, the expectation at work is that it is a place of business, and some things are not appropriate for the workplace.

Rejection

Women are no strangers to stereotypes and being treated differently in many areas of life, and motherhood often adds another dimension to that. It can be particularly frustrating when you are experiencing it from people who knew you before you were a mother. And that treatment can range from almost tiptoeing around you because they no longer think they can relate to brushing you off to assuming you no longer have any interest in anything outside of your kids. It happens in private life with friends whom you may have less in common with, as well as in your professional relationships. Some bosses are supportive, like the one who encouraged me to hire the mom who had been out of the workforce for over a decade. Others, not so much. It takes some time to establish a new normal.

If you feel you are being passed up for opportunities or overlooked because of your perceived lack of time to pursue new challenges, consider a chat with your manager about your career plans. If you are a new mother returning from leave, proactively scheduling a call before you return can help you and your manager align on expectations. Just as you didn't know what to expect before becoming a parent, your manager is also unsure of your mindset when you return. Open communication is always a good place to start. If that fails or you have proof of targeted discrimination, see HR, contact your union rep if applicable, or speak with a lawyer to learn more about your rights.

Resilience

Resilience is the name of the game as a parent! Jokes aside, each stage of parenthood brings joys that you try and hold onto as long as you can, and hardships that you endure until they are over. The resilience to make it through each stage of parenting includes the resilience to adjust your expectations at work to suit the season you are in as a parent.

As I mentioned, volunteering in the kindergarten classroom wasn't my thing. As they got older and into sports, I began volunteering as a coach. Most sports my kids played in elementary school held practices after school, but not AT the school. As a working parent, my husband or I had to leave work to pick them up and take them to another field for an hour-long practice, often forfeiting the money we were spending on after-school care. On a good day, we also remembered all the equipment and even packed a snack! After a season or two, it became clear the only way my husband and I were going to limit the work interruptions was to be able to control the practice times. So our side hustle as volunteer coaches began—soccer, baseball, basketball, and hockey.

It was surprising to learn that telling my coworkers I was leaving early to "coach" little league or basketball, or in my case, ice hockey, garnered more respect from my co-workers, ESPECIALLY my male counterparts. When I said I was off Friday and Monday because I was coaching youth hockey in an away tournament, it was nearly always met positively. My male colleagues wanted to know how I got started in hockey. Have I always played? How was the team doing? No one seemed to worry that I would miss a meeting or needed to move it to accommodate a "coaching responsibility" (see what I did there). This was in contrast to other women who had children with similar sports commitments and were primarily responsible for chauffeuring (not coaching). Those women received annoyed looks from coworkers or comments when they weren't present in meetings that they "were leaving AGAIN " for a kid's sporting event.

Being intentional about your priorities and regularly assessing how things are going at work and home can help keep you on track. To this point, I encourage women to choose the coaching path rather than the chauffeur that so many women end up being. Women have a lot of real value to add in this area. We have as much knowledge, skill, and ability to apply in athletics as we do in the workplace, and it's a gift to pass it along to our kids. It doesn't matter if you didn't play at an "elite" level. Do you think every male Little League coach was a college star? It doesn't take a pro athlete to coach a group of 7-year-olds, and there's no reason why a boys' team shouldn't have a female coach. It takes enthusiasm, patience, and a basic understanding of the game. **And the confidence to believe you belong there! The difference between a man coaching and a woman coaching is that he had the confidence to say "Yes!"** On the off chance that being a coach isn't for you, it's important to shift the mindset from "you have to work at the game" to "you're driving to the game anyway, might as well work it as a coach or scorekeeper or announcer or something."

Reset

In some ways, this particular chapter could have started with reset. Becoming a parent is the biggest reset there is! Everything changes when a child comes into your life. No matter how much you think you are ready, you can't prepare for how your world turns upside down. And the changes keep coming at every stage in your child's development. The newborn phase is different from a nine-month baby, which is different from a toddler, then school age, adolescence—the challenges change, and so must you. It felt like things were changing every six to ten weeks when they were babies, and then when they were older, the distraction of summer vacation, camps, and other holidays that kids get, but parents aren't so lucky. You are constantly resetting as a parent.

Change can be scary, but in this sense, it is an advantage. It can be easy to get stuck in a rut in our careers and in our personal lives, but as our children's developmental stages change, it gives us a chance to reassess our own growth and development. Being a mother and a working woman are not mutually exclusive, and you can be great at both without sacrificing everything. However, it requires you to make the necessary changes to ensure you are getting **the help you need**.

This can include:

- Childcare, both ongoing (such as daycare) and emergency care for sick days, closures, etc.

- Get specific about splitting responsibilities at home. I love a good spreadsheet. Try creating one showing all the things you do in a day/week and review it with people in your circle (partner, parents, friends).

- Streamlining or delegating where appropriate. People do want to help but often don't know the best way to approach offering to help. Sometimes, we rebuff a person's offer because we don't know if they are serious or just being polite—so say "yes" or counter-offer.

- Meal or grocery delivery. If getting to the grocery store with a baby in tow or the thought of making dinner is the drop that spilled the glass, consider automating or outsourcing that process. The delivery fee for groceries often isn't more than a few dollars and is often cheaper than the impulse buys when shopping hungry or tired.

- Reducing the mental load with automated payments, routines, and services that can take mundane but necessary tasks off your hands. Housekeeping or cleaning services. What's affordable? Once a month for the big stuff? Once a week to keep on top of things?

The term "self-care" has become a bit of a code word for spa days, massages, and bubble baths, but real self-care is essential. It is easy to lose oneself in motherhood. Children are demanding, time is tight, and their needs always seem more important than your own. Taking care of your emotional and physical needs is not a luxury, even though it can feel like it when demands are pressing in from all sides. By all means, get a massage because that is self-care, too, but don't stop there. If having groceries delivered makes managing afternoon/evening schedules easier—do it. These things don't have to be forever, only for as long as they make sense. We had landscapers when my kids were babies because it made MY life easier. But once my kids got into middle school, we put it on pause and shifted that responsibility to the kids. It was hard at first to be the only house on the block with little curb appeal, but we called it life skills when they complained that none of their friends had to "trim the hedges."

How many women and mothers don't take a lunch break during the day? True time when they get up, walk away from their desk, go somewhere else and eat, talk, walk, or whatever. It becomes even more important when your free time at home is taken up with parenting. On a personal note, I've noticed that men NEVER skip lunch. And most men leave their desks. They don't scarf down a sandwich hunched over their computer. Working in IT for as long as I have, I know, don't go looking for a guy between 12 - 1 pm; it's a ghost town.

Take care of yourself physically. Daily walks are a start, and then incorporate a time to exercise to clear your head and take care of your body. Remember your interests and make some time for them. For example, you may not be able to sit and read for hours anymore, but a 15-minute reading break daily is a way to honor those parts of you that are still yours. **If you are struggling emotionally, seek help**. Motherhood is an important part of who you are, but it is not all of you. Holding on to some aspects of yourself outside of being a mother is essential.

If your job is no longer meeting your needs, or if you feel that you have shifted professional priorities, consider what type of work would allow you to meet your personal and professional growth goals. Perhaps you could juggle it all when you only had one child but no longer want to work the same number of hours or drive that crazy commute once the second child comes along. I eventually started my own company, partially to balance my work and home life. I no longer wanted to miss one of my kids' games, but I also wasn't interested in giving up my career to become a stay-at-home mom. I don't "have it all," but I have what is most important to me right now. My priorities have changed over the years as the stages of my personal life and family have changed. Yours will, too.

Chapter Summary

- Mothers often put pressure on ourselves to do it all when we need to learn to delegate some things or lean on our support system instead.

- Managing expectations doesn't mean giving up or accepting that we will not be as successful as before. It's understanding that there is a season for everything, and we need to adjust accordingly.

- Societal norms and expectations can be overwhelming, so take time to decide what motherhood will look like for you and shut out the noise.

- The changes that motherhood brings and the different stages your children go through can serve as reminders to reflect on and direct your own professional and personal development regularly.

Conclusion

I was a mentor for a women's networking group for a time. I had six or seven women who were my mentees as part of the program. One of the women wanted to pursue a board role on a board of directors for a non-profit. She was passionate about animals, specifically horses, and a non-profit near her worked with horses that she wanted to be a part of. She thought she had great skills and would be a wonderful addition to the board, which was absolutely true. She had impeccable skills, great work experience and education, and was smart and motivated... so really no doubt in my mind that any organization would be lucky to have her on their board.

When we talked about what she could do to get on the board, in terms of action steps as part of the program's exercise, she said, "I think I want to volunteer with them. Maybe I can start by cleaning some stalls, and then maybe I can grow and help them set up and clean up after their events. Then maybe they'll invite me to be on the board."

I stopped her right there and, a bit tongue in cheek, said, "I don't want you to take offense, but everything you just said? Said no man ever."

Said. No. Man. Ever.

As a mentor, I impressed upon the group that, as women, we often think we need to start at the bottom for whatever reason. This woman had 25 years of work experience, and yet she thought she needed to go and literally shovel horseshit to be qualified to be on their board. I thought that was completely unnecessary. I reminded her that she had value, even if she didn't have the specific experience of working at their particular non-profit. I suggested she go to the board, speak with the executive director, and say, "Hey, I want to be on your board. I have these skills and think I would bring a lot of value to the role."

She struggled with the idea of asking for what she wanted and selling her skills without feeling the need to prove herself first by starting at the bottom. The truth is that you have to make others see your value, and you can't do that if you don't see it first yourself. Women tend to have a harder time seeing their worth than men. Helping women get past that block is one of the reasons I wrote this book.

I've been approached many times in my career by other women asking for advice on something or another, and I've had a few people close to me tell me repeatedly—Write a book! Sharing my stories and advice for thriving as a woman in competitive environments has been something I have been doing in small circles over the course of my career. Ironically, up until three years ago, I had never thought of doing so by writing a book. So, here we are. Much of the career advice given to women is outdated or comes from people with vastly different life experiences and circumstances. For all the times I thought, *That is not the help I need*, I wanted to write a book that would make women say, *This is exactly the help I need!* My career trajectory has mostly been positive, and while my outcome may be uncommon, the obstacles I encountered on my journey are not. I don't like attributing success or failure to luck because I strongly believe that we get out what we put in while acknowledging that, as women, we are often not on an equal playing field.

I often refer to myself as a Title IX baby. Title IX in the United States was enacted to ensure that no person is excluded from participation, denied the benefits of, or discriminated against under any education program or activity that receives Federal funding. In many ways, it leveled the playing field between men and women in academic environments, including school activities such as sports teams. As a result, the number of opportunities for girls and women dramatically increased during my time in academics and sports.

Today, a generation of women have left or are leaving academia with wonderful educational degrees, including more master's degrees than men. In 2020-2021, women earned 62% of all master's degrees and 56% of doctorate degrees in the United States. It institutionalized in women that if we had the GPA, got the A, or aced the test, higher-level academic opportunities would be available based on merit alone. From there came the belief that if we continue to demonstrate similar merit in other institutions, moving to the next level, and the one after that would follow the same merit-based path.

Unfortunately, similar legislation doesn't exist in the workplace, and the path to success is very different from how we progressed through school. Acing the performance review does not necessarily lead to a promotion, and sometimes, those who ace their reviews aren't even the smartest or most talented employees. There are many other skills to learn in the workplace, and the truth is that the playing field is not always equal. Men and women do not always receive the same treatment, and there aren't always equal opportunities for men and women. Being a woman in tech, I'm often outnumbered, even if the gap is closing.

So, what's the solution? Learn to play by the current rules while continuing to work for change. Women are doing great things in the business world despite the barriers they often face. My work as a manager and mentor is often to help women see and believe in their potential, and to chase opportunities as aggressively and opportunistically as their male counterparts.

As you move forward in your career path, I want you to keep returning to the big three:

Why not me?

If not me, then who?

If not now, when?

Why Not Me?

Seriously, **why not you?** Why aren't you heading up that project, applying for that promotion, or starting your own business? Women tend to lack the confidence they need to push forward and make those leaps in ways that men often do without thinking twice about it. We tend to look at people who are doing incredible things as though they are somehow in a different league or have some magic ingredient we don't have. It's just not true. Yes, some people are lucky to start life in a privileged financial situation or have connections, but you don't need those to pursue your dreams. My career path went from girl-next-door to CEO through hard work, passion, and a belief in myself. Yours can, too.

If Not Me, Then Who?

Which of your colleagues is better suited to what you're afraid to go after? Which has their life in perfect order, their qualifications perfectly aligned, and their skillset a perfect match? Anybody? And if they do, why aren't they already in the role you want?

Tangible skills and qualifications are worth something, but they're not everything. If you keep comparing yourself to everyone around you, you'll end up in a state of paralysis, where you're afraid to move on from what is comfortable and certain. Only certainty is an illusion. Companies reorganize, downsize, or simply shut down. New managers come in and shake things up. Sometimes, an employee is a target simply because they are too much of an institution and are seen as an obstacle to modernizing practices. Which of your colleagues are guaranteed to be safe in a company shake-up? Probably none.

I started my own company after asking myself *If not me, then who?* That decision to keep going professionally and start my own company took a lot of courage on my part, but I don't regret it for a minute. It set a strong example for my children that I didn't realize until much later. They have witnessed the highs and lows of that risk firsthand. At the same time, they still get to see me as their number-one fan. I regained my excitement for my career and now get the chance to put into practice all the lessons I've learned that I've shared with you in this book.

Stop watching your friends and colleagues achieve the goals you want for yourself. Put yourself out there, and brush off failures as experience. Or you risk getting stuck in the double-sided coin of being paralyzed by imposter syndrome or the need to be perfect. Don't let a lack of perfect circumstances hold you back. **If not you, then who?**

If Not Now, When?

If you're waiting to be perfectly qualified, you may be waiting a long time. If you're waiting for the perfect circumstances, you'll be waiting forever. There's always a reason why not to do something, why it's never the right time. Before you know it, next year becomes five, and there's something else in the way. **If not now, when?**

If you can't take a huge leap, take the first step. Though I'll be honest, most women are more than ready to take the huge leap; they're simply afraid to. Don't let life pass you by out of fear. Use the skills in this book to go after what you want.

Rather than wait until the magical "right time," I believe that you should be actively planning to move toward the career you want by taking action steps to make it happen. I often get asked about how I started my company. Specifically, how I went from project manager to CEO. The idea of working for yourself is a very romantic one for many, so I have counseled countless women in this area.

My advice to them and you is to stop thinking about a theoretical future plan and figure out what risk you could take now that you have been avoiding out of fear and not because it isn't doable. For every five women who realize entrepreneurship is not for them, there is one who is completely energized by our conversation and realizes she has been more than ready to take that step for a long time.

Watching those women take the leap is an incredible experience. But so is watching the other women realize their real dreams and find the courage to begin pursuing them instead of holding on to one that doesn't suit them.

The path to success is not linear. Even the most successful people fail. I have shared some of my personal stories of resetting my path to illustrate the point. If you give up every time you fail, you will never succeed at much. Each time you go through this cycle, you will get closer to your goals and the life you deserve. The world of work changes so quickly. You shouldn't wait for a career to *develop*; you need to *empower* it!

Take a risk. Prepare for rejection. Practice resilience while you regroup. Reset your goals and start again.

Take a risk!

This is the help you need.

About the Author

Tiffany Rosik, CEO of TGR Management Consulting and trusted advisor to Fortune 1000 companies, tackles complex projects by fostering high-performing teams that deliver results. Tiffany is passionate about helping women achieve their full workplace potential by serving as a Mentor, Coach, and Leader. Her book bridges the theory-practice gap, empowering women to thrive in the real world. Tiffany holds a Master's in Information Systems from Loyola University Chicago and a Bachelor of Science in Marketing from Millikin University, as well as numerous certifications.

References

Agovino, T. (2023, March 15). *The performance review problem.* SHRM. https://www.shrm.org/topics-tools/news/hr-magazine/performance-review-problem

Babcock, L., Laschever, S. (2007). *Women Don't Ask: The High Cost of Avoiding Negotiation--and Positive Strategies for Change.* New York: Bantam Books.

Babcock, L., Peyser, B., Vesterlund, L., & Weingart, L. (2022). *The No Club: putting a stop to women's dead-end work.* Simon and Schuster.

Borden, T. (2024, February 19). *Career breaks are different for women- Here's what happens when they come back.* LinkedIn News. https://www.linkedin.com/pulse/career-breaks-different-women-heres-what-happens-when-taylor-borden-25oye/

CBI Catalyzing Corporation. (n.d.). *CBI's mutual gains approach to negotiation.* https://www.cbi.org/article/mutual-gains-approach/

Coy, P. (2023, August 18). *Opinion: The hidden risk of getting paid in stock options.* The New York Times Subscriber-Only Newsletter. https://www.nytimes.com/2023/08/18/opinion/stock-options-start-ups.html

Dickler, J. (Updated 2023, September 7). *Women will accept $66,000 a year to take a new job- while men hold out for more than $90,000.* CNBC. https://www.cnbc.com/2023/09/06/gender-pay-gap-womens-salary-expectations-are-25k-lower-than-mens.html

Eckstein, AJ. (2023, August 6). *I interviewed 30 recruiters and here are the 7 biggest lessons I've learned about landing a job.* Fast Company. https://www.fastcompany.com/90906476/7-lessons-ive-learned-about-landing-a-job#:~:text=And%20researchers%20have%20found%20that,proceeding%20to%20the%20interviewing%20stage.

Elsesser, K. (2023, November 2). *Women more likely to negotiate salaries but still earn less than men, research says.* Forbes. https://www.forbes.com/sites/kimelsesser/2023/11/02/women-more-likely-to-negotiate-salaries-but-still-earn-less-than-men-research-says/?sh=100a3b15e8b0

Ford, K. (2010, April 29). *To plan your career, think chutes and ladders.* Bits of Kelly. https://kellynford.com/2010/04/29/to-plan-your-career-path-think-chutes-and-ladders/#:~:text=Chutes%20represent%20continuity%20%26%20%20transferring%20skills,more%20options%20in%20the%20future

Gitis, B., Sprick, E., Schweer, A. (2022, February 11). BPC-Morning consult: 1 in 5 moms experience pregnancy discrimination in the workplace. Bipartisan Policy Center. https://bipartisanpolicy.org/blog/bpc-morning-consult-pregnancy-discrimination/#:~:text=Nearly%201%20in%204%20mothers,pregnancy%20discrimination%20in%20the%20workplace.

Gurchiek, K. (2017, February 3). *Conducting performance reviews? Get out the tissues.* SHRM. https://www.shrm.org/topics-tools/news/conducting-performance-reviews-get-tissues

HRD. (archived). *The pros and cons of offering employee stock options.* https://www.hcamag.com/ca/archived/the-pros-and-cons-of-offering-employee-stock-options/127502

Hsu, A. (2023, April 13). *Women are earning more money. But they're still picking up a heavier load at home.* NPR. https://www.npr.org/2023/04/13/1168961388/pew-earnings-gender-wage-gap-housework-chores-child-care

Indeed Editorial Team. (Updated 2022, November 6). *Toxic leadership (With definition and a list of traits).* Indeed. https://ca.indeed.com/career-advice/career-development/toxic-leadership

Johnivan, J. R. (2023, December 11). The latest performance management statistics (2024 update). Select Software Reviews. https://www.selectsoftwarereviews.com/blog/performance-management-statistics#:~:text=According%20to%20SHRM%2C%2071%25%20of,reviews%20for%20their%20respective%20teams.

Lança, M. (2023, July 24). *Essential Employee Management Statistics in 2023.* Folks. https://folksrh.com/en/blog/performance-management-statistics/

National Center for Education Statistics. (Updated 2023, May). *Graduate Degree Fields.* https://nces.ed.gov/programs/coe/indicator/ctb/graduate-degree-fields

Perry, E. (2021, June 2). *The 8 toxic leadership traits (and how to spot them).* Better Up. https://www.betterup.com/blog/8-toxic-leadership-traits-to-avoid-plus-how-to-spot-them

Shortlister Editorial Team. (n.d.). *50+ Maternity leave statistics in 2024.* Shortlister. https://www.myshortlister.com/insights/maternity-leave-statistics

Tenney, M. (n.d.). *The 5 leadership styles most commonly utilized.* Business Leadership Today. https://businessleadershiptoday.com/what-are-the-5-leadership-styles/

The Global Financial Literacy Excellence Center (GFLEC). (2021, March 8). *Lack of confidence accounts for one-third of financial literacy gender gap.* PR Newswire. https://www.prnewswire.com/news-releases/lack-of-confidence-accounts-for-one-third-of-financial-literacy-gender-gap-301241834.html

Their, J. (2022, December 17). *Women and men ask for raises the same amount. You can probably guess who gets them more often.* Fortune. https://fortune.com/2022/12/17/women-men-ask-for-raises-at-same-rate/

U.S. Department of Education. (Revised 2021, August). *Title IX and sex discrimination.* Office for Civil Rights. https://www2.ed.gov/about/offices/list/ocr/docs/tix_dis.html

www.ingramcontent.com/pod-product-compliance
Lightning Source LLC
Chambersburg PA
CBHW071208210326
41597CB00016B/1722